THE ROYAL COURT THEATRE in association with
THE ROYAL NATIONAL THEATRE STUDIO presents

TOAST

by Richard Bean

First performed at the Royal Court Theatre Upstairs
West Street, London WC2 on 12th February 1999

Sponsored by the Jerwood Foundation

JERWOOD
NEW PLAYWRIGHTS

The Royal Court is delighted that the relationship with the Jerwood
Foundation which started in 1993 is to continue this season with their
support of TOAST, LIFT OFF, TRUST and SACRED HEART. The
Foundation's commitment to supporting new plays by new playwrights has
contributed to some of the Royal Court's most successful productions in
recent years, including THE STEWARD OF CHRISTENDOM, MOJO,
SHOPPING AND FUCKING, EAST IS EAST, THE BEAUTY QUEEN OF
LEENANE, THE WEIR and REAL CLASSY AFFAIR.

The Jerwood Foundation is a private foundation, dedicated to imaginative
and responsible funding of the arts, education and many other areas of
human endeavour and excellence, particularly inititatives supporting young
talent. In addition to sponsorships such as Jerwood New Playwrights, the
Foundation has opened the Jerwood Space, a new arts centre in central
London offering low-cost rehearsal and production facilities for young
drama and dance groups and art gallery space for emerging artists.

The Beauty Queen of Leenane
by Martin McDonagh
(Photograph: Ivan Kyncl)

The Weir by Conor McPherson
(Photograph: Ivan Kyncl)

East is East by Ayub Khan-Din
(Photograph: Robert Day)

Real Classy Affair by Nick Grosso
(Photograph: Henry Bond)

TOAST
by Richard Bean

Cast

Lance, the 'Student', 2nd Oven Man Christopher Campbell
Colin, the Spare Wank Ian Dunn
Peter, the Tinner Up Matthew Dunster
Walter Nelson (Nellie), the Mixer Ewan Hooper
Cecil, the Tinman on the Prover Sam Kelly
Blakey, the Chargehand Mark Williams
Dezzie, 1st Oven Man Paul Wyett

Director Richard Wilson
Designer Julian McGowan
Lighting Designer Johanna Town
Sound Designer Paul Arditti
Assistant Director Ryan Romain
Production Manager Paul Handley
Company Stage Manager Cath Binks
Stage Managers Pea Horsley, Kirsteen O'Kane and Emma Laxton
Costume Supervisor Susan Coates
Dialect Coach Joan Washington
Set Construction Andrew Beauchamp

The Royal Court Theatre would like to thank the following for their help with this production: Wardrobe care by Persil and Comfort courtesy of Lever Brothers Ltd; refrigerators by Electrolux and Philips Major Appliances Ltd; kettles by Morphy Richards; video for casting purposes by Hitachi; backstage coffee machine by West 9; furniture by Knoll International; freezer for backstage use supplied by Zanussi Ltd 'Now that's a good idea.'; Closed circuit TV cameras and monitors by Mitsubishi UK Ltd; Natural spring water from Aqua Cool, 12 Waterside Way, London SW17 0XH, tel. 0181-947 5666; Overhead projector from W.H. Smith; backstage microwave supplied by Sanyo U.K; Watford Palace Theatre

The Company

Richard Bean (writer)
Richard Bean worked in a Bread Plant from 1974 - 75 and was a stand-up comedian between 1989 and 1994.
Opera includes: Libretto for Stephen McNeff's Paradise of Fools (Unicorn Arts Theatre)
Radio includes: Of Rats and Men (Radio 4); Control Group Six (Radio 4) as co-writer / performer.

Paul Arditti (sound designer)
Paul has been designing sound for theatre since 1983. He currently combines his post as Head of Sound at the Royal Court Theatre (where he has designed more than forty productions) with regular freelance projects.
For the Royal Court, Paul's designs include: The Kitchen, Rat in the Skull, Some Voices, Mojo, The Lights, The Weir; The Steward of Christendom, Shopping and Fucking, Blue Heart (co-productions with Out of Joint); The Chairs (co-production with Theatre de Complicite); The Strip, Never Land, Cleansed, Via Dolorosa, Real Classy Affair, 1998 Young Writers' Festival 'Choice' and The Glory of Living.
Among Paul's other credits are many productions with the Royal National Theatre, including Our Lady of Sligo (with Out of Joint). For the Royal Shakespeare Company, recent work includes Hamlet and The Tempest. On Broadway Paul's work won him a Drama Desk Award for Outstanding Sound Design in 1992, for the music theatre piece Four Baboons Adoring The Sun, and he was delighted to have been nominated again last year for his work on Simon McBurney's acclaimed production of The Chairs. In the West End, Paul's designs include Orpheus Descending, Cyrano de Bergerac, St Joan.
Musicals include: Doctor Dolittle, Piaf, The Threepenny Opera.

Christopher Campbell
Theatre includes: Macbeth, Dragon, Pygmalion, The Night of the Iguana, Jo-Jo the Melon Donkey, The Franklin's Tale, Mary Stuart, Oedipus the King, Oedipus at Colonnus, Flight (Royal National Theatre); What Every Woman Knows (West Yorkshire Playhouse); Purgatory in Ingolstadt, Pioneers in Ingolstadt (Gate, London); Translations, All My Sons (Birmingham Rep); A Midsummer Nights Dream (Globe, Canada); Black Ice, Robin Hood (Derby Playhouse); Dr Faustus, Christie in Love (Vox Touring Theatre); Beaux Stratagem, As You Like It (Engligh Touring Theatre); Reader (Traverse); Communicating Doors (Library, Manchester).
Television includes: Coasting, Families, Sherlock Holmes and the Missing Link, World in Action, Confessional.

Ian Dunn
For the Royal Court: I Am Yours, Babies, Six Degrees of Separation (& Comedy).
Other theatre includes: Chips With Everything, Somewhere (RNT); Our Boys (Donmar / Derby Playhouse); A Prayer For Wings (Tour); Hidden Laughter (Vaudeville); Forget-Me-Not-Lane (Greenwich); Invisible Friends, Wolf At The Door, Brighton Beach Memoirs (Scarborough).
Television includes: Bliss, Stone Scissors Paper, Shine On Harvey Moon, Casualty, Desmonds, Jackanory, The Merrihill Millionaires, The Bill, A Touch of Frost, Soldier Soldier, Children Of The North, Sweet Capital Lives, The Saturday Night Armistice.
Film includes: American Friends, Bye Bye Baby.

Matthew Dunster
Theatre includes: The Outsider, The Trial, The Mill On The Floss (Contact); But The Living Are Wrong In The Sharp Distinctions They Make, Nest of Spices, The Wasp Factory, (Newcastle Playhouse); Tales From The Magic Story Bowl (Bolton Octagon); Happy Families (Derby); Road (Royal Exchange); Fallen Angels (Fecund); Flying (RNT Studio).
Television includes: Spring Hill, Brookside, New Voices, Golden Collar, Into the Fire, Walking On The Moon.
As a writer: You Used To (Contact); Tell Me (Contact, Newcastle Playhouse, Donmar Warehouse); The Glazier (European Tour with P.I.E.T.A.).
Matthew is currently under commission to the Royal Exchange Theatre, Manchester.

Ewan Hooper
For the Royal Court: Bingo, Falkland Sound / Gibraltar Strait, All Things Nice, Hammett's
Apprentice, The Kitchen, The Changing Room, Blue Heart (with Out of Joint).
Other theatre includes: Henry V, Coriolanus, The Broken Heart, The Caretaker (RSC);
Roots (RNT); She Stoops to Conquer, The Doctor's Dilemma, The Recruiting Officer, Richard
II, Much Ado about Nothing, Hindle Wakes (Royal Exchange, Manchester); The Woman in
Black (Fortune Theatre).
Television includes: The Rules that Jack Made, Hunters Walk, King Lear, Hi-de-Hi, Invasion,
Across the Lake.
Film includes: How I Won The War, Julius Caesar, Personal Sevices.

Sam Kelly
For the Royal Court: This Is A Chair, Killers, Inventing A New Colour (& Bristol Old Vic),
Party People (Young Writers' Festival '98)
Other theatre includes: Le Bourgeois Gentilhomme (Edinburgh Festival '97); The
Homecoming, War and Peace, Pericles (RNT); Dead Funny (Savoy); The Madras House
(Lyceum Edinburgh, Lyric Hammersmith); Wallflowering, Last of the Red Hot Lovers (West
Yorkshire Playhouse); The Odd Couple (Royal Exchange Manchester); Dangerous Obsession
(Fortune); 'Allo 'Allo (Prince of Wales); Run For Your Wife (Criterion); The Government
Inspector (Royal Exchange); The Two Ronnies Stage Show (London Palladium & Australia)
Television includes: Barbara, Cold Feet, Magic With Everything, Holding On, Born To Run,
Dressing For Breakfast, Paul Merton in Twelve Angry Men, Impasse, Of Sound Mind, A Touch
of Frost, 11 Men Against 11, Martin Chuzzlewit, Stalag Luft, Young Indy, Stay Lucky, On The
Up, Voice, Blood Rights, Haggard, Making Out, Home To Roost, Christabel, Thin Air, Victoria
Wood Special, Will You Still Love Me Tomorrow, Heart Of The Country, Frankie & Johnnie,
Hold The Back Page, Jenny's War, Bleak House, 'Allo 'Allo, Dave Allen, Coronation Street,
Boys From The Black Stuff, Now And Then, Professional Foul, Grown Ups.
Film includes: Untitled '98 (Mike Leigh), Getaway, Blue Ice, Arthur's Hallowed Ground
Radio includes: occasional presenter for Listening Corner (Radio 4) ; Le Bourgeois
Gentilhomme, Babblewick Hall, Strong Language, England's Glory, Uncle Mort's Celtic Fringe,
Knocking on Heaven's Door (BBC).

Julian McGowan (designer)
For the Royal Court: American Bagpipes, The Treatment, The Censor.
For the Royal Court with Out of Joint: The Steward of Christendom, Blue Heart.
Other theatre includes: Don Juan, The Lodger, Women Laughing (Royal Exchange,
Manchester); The Possibilities, The LA Plays, Venice Preserved (Almeida); The Rivals, Man and
Superman, Playboy of the Western World, Hedda Gabler (Citizens); The Changling,The
Wives' Excuse (RSC); Caesar and Cleopatra, Total Eclipse, A Tale of Two Cities (Greenwich
Theatre).
Opera designs include: Cosi Fan Tutte (New Israeli Opera); Eugene Onegin (Scottish Opera);
Siren Song (Almeida Opera Festival).

Johanna Town (lighting designer)
Johanna has been Head of Lighting for the Royal Court since 1990 and has designed
extensively for the company during this time. Productions include: The Kitchen, Faith Healer,
Pale Horse, Search and Destroy, Women Laughing, Never Land. Most recent freelance
credits include: Little Malcolm (Hampstead and West End); Our Country's Good (Young Vic /
Out of Joint); Our Lady Of Sligo (National Theatre / Out Of Joint); Blue Heart (New York /
Out Of Joint); Shopping And Fucking (The Queens & New York); Afore Night Come (Theatre
Clywd); The Misfits (Royal Exchange).
Opera includes: La Boheme, Die Fledermaus (MTL); Ottello and The Marriage of Figaro
(Opera Du Nice)
Johanna is currently working on the refurbishment of the Royal Court in Sloane Square.

Mark Williams

For the Royal Court: The Plague Year, William (Young Writers' Festival).

Other theatre as an actor includes: The Fast Show Live on Stage (Apollo); Art (Wyndhams); A Dream of People, Moscow Gold, Singer, As You Like It (RSC); The City Wives Confederacy (Greenwich); Doctor of Honour (Cheek By Jowl); Fanshen (RNT); Everyman (Upstream)

Theatre as an director includes: Bleeding Hearts, In Exile (Riverside Studios)

Television includes: Ted & Ralph, Hunting Venus, The Fast Show, Searching, Peak Practice, The Big Game, Chef, 99-1, Health and Efficiency, Casualty, The Honeymoon's Over, Bad Company, Kinsey, Harry Enfield's Television Programme, Stuff, Making Out, Red Dwarf, Tumbledown, Coppers, The Trial.

Film includes: Shakespeare In Love, The Borrowers, 101 Dalmations.

Richard Wilson (director)

For the Royal Court as a director: Four (Young Writers' Festival '98), Other Worlds, Heaven and Hell, A Wholly Healthy Glasgow, Women Laughing (both originally at the Royal Exchange, Manchester), God's Second In Command,

For the Royal Court as an actor: Operation Bad Apple, An Honourable Trade, May Days.

Richard Wilson has numerous other credits for theatre, film and television as both an actor and a director. He most recently directed Tom and Clem which ran in the West End. His most recent work as an actor is the film The Man Who Knew Too Little, the LWT sitcom Duck Patrol, and he has just completed filming on the BBC series Life Support.

In 1994 he was awarded the OBE for services to drama as a director and actor.

Paul Wyett

For the Royal Court: My Hearts a Suitcase (Young Writers' Festival '91), Class (Young Writers' Festival '98).

Other theatre includes: Seeing Red (B.A.C.); Dealers Choice (West Yorkshire Playhouse); Bad Company (Bush); Billy Liar, Murmuring Judges, Arturo Ui (RNT); Bad Company, Fanta Babies, Price of Coal (RNT Studio); Space (Soho Poly Theatre).

Television includes: Heartbeat, Accused, Pie In The Sky, Out of the Blue, Hand Gliding, First of the Summer Wine.

Film includes: A Soldier's Tale.

THE ENGLISH STAGE COMPANY
AT THE ROYAL COURT THEATRE

The English Stage Company was formed to bring serious writing back to the stage. The first Artistic Director, George Devine, wanted to create a vital and popular theatre. He encouraged new writing that explored subjects drawn from contemporary life as well as pursuing European plays and forgotten classics. When John Osborne's Look Back in Anger was first produced in 1956, it forced British theatre into the modern age. In addition to plays by 'angry young men', the international repertoire included Bertolt Brecht, Eugène Ionesco, Jean-Paul Sartre, Marguerite Duras, Frank Wedekind and Samuel Beckett.

The ambition was to discover new work which was challenging, innovative and of the highest quality, underpinned by a contemporary style of presentation. Early Court writers included Arnold Wesker, John Arden, Ann Jellicoe, N F Simpson, Edward Bond and David Storey. They were followed by David Hare, Howard Brenton, Caryl Churchill, Timberlake Wertenbaker, Robert Holman and Jim Cartwright. Many of their plays are now modern classics.

Many established playwrights had their early plays produced in the Theatre Upstairs including Anne Devlin, Andrea Dunbar, Sarah Daniels, Jim Cartwright, Clare McIntyre, Winsome Pinnock, Martin Crimp and Phyllis Nagy. Since 1994 there has been a succession of plays by writers new to the Royal Court, many of them first plays, produced in association with the Royal National Theatre Studio with sponsorship from the Jerwood Foundation. The writers include Joe Penhall, Nick Grosso, Judy Upton, Sarah Kane, Michael Wynne, Judith Johnson, James Stock, Simon Block and Mark Ravenhill. Since 1996 the Jerwood New Playwrights Series has supported new plays by Jez Butterworth, Martin McDonagh and Ayub Khan-Din (in the Theatre Downstairs), and by Mark Ravenhill, Tamantha Hammerschlag, Jess Walters, Conor McPherson, Meredith Oakes and Rebecca Prichard (in the Theatre Upstairs).

The Spring 1999 season is again presented in association with the Royal National Theatre Studio, including playwrights Rebecca Gilman, Richard Bean, Roy Williams, Gary Mitchell and Mick Mahoney. The last four also form part of the Jerwood New Playwrights series.

Theatre Upstairs productions regularly transfer to the Theatre Downstairs, as with Ariel Dorfman's Death and the Maiden, Sebastian Barry's The Steward of Christendom (a co-production with Out of Joint), Martin McDonagh's The Beauty Queen Of Leenane (a co-production with Druid Theatre Company), Ayub Khan-Din's East is East (a co-production with Tamasha Theatre Company). Some Theatre Upstairs productions transfer to the West End, such as Kevin Elyot's My Night With Reg, Mark Ravenhill's Shopping and Fucking (a co-production with Out of Joint) and Conor McPherson's The Weir.

1992-1998 have been record-breaking years at the box-office with capacity houses for Death and the Maiden, Six Degrees of Separation, Oleanna, Hysteria, The Cavalcaders, The Kitchen, The Queen & I, The Libertine, Simpatico, Mojo, The Steward of Christendom, The Beauty Queen of Leenane, East is East, The Chairs, Real Classy Affair and The Weir.

Now in its temporary homes, the Duke of York's and Ambassadors Theatres, during the refurbishment of its Sloane Square theatre, the Royal Court continues to present the best in new work. After four decades the company's aims remain consistent with those established by George Devine. The Royal Court is still a major focus in the country for the production of new work. Scores of plays first seen at the Royal Court are now part of the national and international dramatic repertoire.

The Royal Court Theatre is financially assisted by the Royal Borough of Kensington and Chelsea. Recipient of a grant from the Theatre Restoration Fund & from the Foundation for Sport & the Arts. The Royal Court's Play Development Programme is funded by the A.S.K. Theater Projects. Supported by the National Lottery through the Arts Council of England. Royal Court Registered Charity number 231242.

AWARDS FOR THE ROYAL COURT THEATRE

Death and the Maiden and Six Degrees of Separation won the Olivier Award for Best Play in 1992 and 1993 respectively. Hysteria won the 1994 Olivier Award for Best Comedy, and also the Writers' Guild Award for Best West End Play. My Night with Reg won the 1994 Writers' Guild Award for Best Fringe Play, the Evening Standard Award for Best Comedy, and the 1994 Olivier Award for Best Comedy. Sebastian Barry won the 1995 Writers' Guild Award for Best Fringe Play, the 1995 Critics' Circle Award and the 1997 Christopher Ewart-Biggs Literary Prize for The Steward of Christendom, and the 1995 Lloyds Private Banking Playwright of the Year Award. Jez Butterworth won the 1995 George Devine Award for Most Promising Playwright, the 1995 Writers' Guild New Writer of the Year Award, the Evening Standard Award for Most Promising Playwright and the 1995 Olivier Award for Best Comedy for Mojo. Phyllis Nagy won the 1995 Writers' Guild Award for Best Regional Play for Disappeared.

Michael Wynne won the 1996 Meyer-Whitworth Award for The Knocky. Martin McDonagh won the 1996 George Devine Award, the1996 Writers' Guild Best Fringe Play Award, the 1996 Critics' Circle Award and the 1996 Evening Standard Award for Most Promising Playwright for The Beauty Queen of Leenane. Marina Carr won the 19th Susan Smith Blackburn Prize (1996/7) for Portia Coughlan. Conor McPherson won the 1997 George Devine Award, the 1997 Critics' Circle Award and the 1997 Evening Standard Award for Most Promising Playwright for The Weir. Ayub Khan-Din won the 1997 Writers' Guild Award for Best West End Play, the 1997 Writers' Guild New Writer of the Year Award and the 1996 John Whiting Award for East is East. Anthony Neilson won the 1997 Writers' Guild Award for Best Fringe Play for The Censor. The Royal Court was the overall winner of the 1995 Prudential Award for the Arts for creativity, excellence, innovation and accessibility. The Royal Court Theatre Upstairs won the 1995 Peter Brook Empty Space Award for innovation and excellence in theatre.

At the 1998 Tony Awards, The Beauty Queen of Leenane (co-production with Druid Theatre Company) won four awards including Garry Hynes for Best Director and was nominated for a further two. The Chairs (co-production with Theatre de Complicite) was also nominated for six awards. In 1998 Taormina Arte awarded the European prize New Theatrical Realities to the Royal Court for its efforts in recent years to discover and promote the work of young British dramatists. In the Time Out Live Awards of December 1998, David Hare won the award for Outstanding Achievement for Via Dolorosa, produced by the Royal Court in September. Sarah Kane won the 1998 Arts Foundation Fellowship in Playwriting and Rebecca Prichard won the 1998 Critics Circle Award for most Promising Playwright.

THE ROYAL COURT THEATRE BOOKSHOP

Located in the foyer of the Duke of York's Theatre, St Martin's Lane, the Royal Court Theatre bookshop is open most afternoons and evenings until after the evening performance. It holds a wide range of theatre books, playtexts and film scripts - over 1,000 titles in all. Many Royal Court Theatre playtexts are available for just £2. Among these are the recent productions of:

The Glory of Living - Rebecca Gilman, The Weir - Conor McPherson, Real Classy Affair - Nick Grosso, The Old Neighborhood - David Mamet, Gas Station Angel - Ed Thomas, Yard Gal - Rebecca Prichard, Been So Long - Che Walker, Cleansed - Sarah Kane, I Am Yours - Judith Thompson, The Chairs - Eugène Ionesco, Never Land - Phyllis Nagy, Blue Heart - Caryl Churchill, The Censor - Anthony Neilson, East is East - Ayub Khan-Din, The Beauty Queen of Leenane - Martin McDonagh, Shopping and Fucking - Mark Ravenhill

The bookshop also sells polo shirts, record bags, mugs and chocolate. Telephone enquiries can be made directly to the Bookshop Manager, Del Campbell, on: 0171 565 5024.

THE ROYAL NATIONAL THEATRE STUDIO

The Studio is the centre of research and development for the National - an important seedbed for growth and experiment in British theatre today. It provides a workspace outside the confines of the rehearsal room and stage where artists can experiment and develop their skills. Central to the Studio's work is a commitment to new writing; work developed there reaches audiences throughout the country and overseas, on radio, film and television, as well as at the National and other theatres in London - as with this season of plays with the Royal Court. Web site: www.nt-online.org

Studio

FRIENDS OF THE ROYAL COURT

You can see every Royal Court play for only £5 by becoming a Royal Court Friend. By joining the Friends scheme, you will receive:

- advance information and priority booking at the opening of each season.

- two seats for every production in both the Theatre Upstairs and Downstairs for only £5.

- Free tickets for all the Royal Court's public readings of new plays from around the world.

- an exclusive newsletter keeping you close to the heart of the world's leading new writing theatre.

Annual membership of the Royal Court Friends is only £20 (with an initial one-off joining fee of £25). To join, simply send a cheque or postal order (made payable to English Stage Company) or your credit card details to Friends Memberships, Royal Court Theatre, St Martins Lane, London WC2N 4BG. For more information, contact the Box Office on 0171 565 5000.

FREE MAILING LIST

Call our free mailing list hotline on **0906 5500 666** and receive priority information about new Royal Court productions and special events. *(calls are charged at £1/min and should last no more than one minute).* You can also join our e-mailing list and receive news of our latest web site updates by sending the message 'subscribe list' to **marketing@ royal-court.demon.co.uk.** The Royal Court's web site can be found at **www.royal-court.org.uk**

RE-BUILDING THE ROYAL COURT

The Royal Court was thrilled in 1995 to be awarded a National Lottery grant through the Arts Council of England, to pay for three quarters of a £26 million project to re-build completely our 100-year old home. The rules of the award required the Royal Court to raise £7 million as partnership funding. Thanks to the generous support of the donors listed below and a recent major donation from the Jerwood Foundation, we have very nearly reached the target. The building work is near completion at the Sloane Square site and the theatre is due to reopen in Autumn 1999.

With only £300,000 left to raise, each donation makes a significant difference to the realisation of this exciting project: for example a donation of £20 pays for 40 bricks, £100 pays for two square metres of reclaimed timber flooring and £1,000 enables you to 'name' a seat in the re-built Theatre. If you would like to help, or for further information, please contact Royal Court Development on 0171 565 5050.

ROYAL COURT DEVELOPMENT BOARD

Elisabeth Murdoch (Chair), Timothy Burrill, Anthony Burton, Jonathan Cameron, Jonathan Caplin QC, Victoria Elenowitz, Monica Gerard-Sharp, Susan Hayden, Angela Heylin, Feona McEwan, Sue Stapely, Charlotte Watcyn Lewis

RE-BUILDING SUPPORTERS
Jerwood Foundation

WRITERS CIRCLE
BSkyB Ltd
News International plc
Pathé
The Eva and Hans K Rausing Trust
The Rayne Foundation
Garfield Weston Foundation

DIRECTORS CIRCLE
The Granada Group plc
John Lewis Partnership plc

ACTORS CIRCLE
Quercus Charitable Trust
RSA Art for Architecture Award Scheme
The Basil Samuel Charitable Trust
The Trusthouse Charitable Foundation
The Woodward Charitable Trust

STAGE HANDS CIRCLE
Anonymous
The Arthur Andersen Foundation
Associated Newspapers Ltd
The Honorable M L Astor Charitable Trust
Rosalind Bax
Character Masonry Services Ltd
Elizabeth Corob
Toby Costin
Double O Charity
Lindy Fletcher
Michael Frayn
Mr R Hopkins
Roger Jospe
William Keeling
Lex Service plc

Fiona McCall
Mr J Mills
Jimmy Mulville and Denise O'Donoghue
David Murby
J Orr
Michael Orr
William Poeton CBE and Barbara Poeton
Angela Pullen
Ann Scurfield
Ricky Shuttleworth
Mr N Trimble
Richard Wilson
Mrs Katherine Yates

STAGE HANDS DONORS
Anonymous
P Abel Smith
Mr Graham Billing
Mr M Bishton
Chubb Insurance Company of Europe SA
CT Bowring
A Corson
Jess Cully
Sir Evelyn de Rothschild
Mr and Mrs Greene
Margaret Guido Charitable Trust
Mrs T Harris
Mr S Hanbold
Ian Holm CBE
Catherine Holmes à Court
Dr A V Jones
Mr H Kappen
Mrs L Lee
Lady Lever
Mrs A Mastrovito
James Midgley
Steve Mole
Eva Monley
Martin Newson
Barbara Nokes

Northbridge Charitable Trust
Mrs Posgate
Schroder Charity Trust
Mr Harry Streets
Mr Weatherstone
Mr Timothy West
And over 3,500 more audience members and supporters

SEAT PATRONS
Anonymous
Judith Asalache
Michael Astor
BBC1
BBC2
Trevor Bentham
Lily Bourne
Friends of Margaret Branch
Sally Burton
Harold Cantor
Lily Cantor
Gerard Casey
Amber Currie
Daisy Currie
David Day
Simone Fenton
Thomas Fenton
Gordon Flemyng
In memory of Carl Forgione 1944 - 1998
In memory of Bill Fournier
Elsie Fowler
Charlotte Fraser
Nicholas Fraser
Anita Frew

Lisa Goodhew
Thomas Goodhew
Nigel Hawthorne
Pola Jones
Gemma Kingsbury
Jake Kingsbury
Toby Kingsbury
Benjamin Lebus
Joseph Lebus
Samuel Lebus
Beatrix Lehmann
David Marks
Max Factor
Alec McCowen
Nicola McFarland
Sam Melluish
Barbara Minto
Bill Newall
Phyl Newall
Georgia Oetker
Arlene Phillips
Pauline Pinder
André Ptaszynski
April Robinson
Richard Robinson
Samantha Robinson
Timothy Robinson
Sarah and Louise Roeder
Pam and Jim Rose
Phoebe Saatchi
Fiona Shaw
Brook Sinclair
In memory of Norman Joshua Swift
Sally Swift
Gwen Taylor
Tomkins plc
Nicholas Warren

PROGRAMME SUPPORTERS

The Royal Court (English Stage Company Ltd) is supported financially by a wide range of private companies and public bodies and earns the remainder of its income from the Box Office and its own trading activities.

The company receives its principal funding from the Arts Council of England, which has supported the Court since 1956. The Royal Borough of Kensington & Chelsea gives an annual grant to the Royal Court Young People's Theatre and the London Boroughs Grants Committee contributes to the cost of productions in its Theatre Upstairs.

Other parts of the company's activities are made possible by sponsorship and private foundation support: 1993 saw the start of its association with the A.S.K. Theater Projects of Los Angeles, which is funding a Playwrights Programme at the Royal Court. In 1999 the Jerwood Foundation continues to support the production of new plays by new writers with the fourth series of Jerwood New Playwrights. Last year we also welcomed Bloomberg Mondays, a continuation of the Royal Court's reduced price ticket scheme, now generously supported by Bloomberg News.

We are grateful to all our supporters for their vital and on-going commitment.

TRUSTS AND FOUNDATIONS
Jerwood Foundation
Alan & Babette
 Sainsbury Charitable Fund
The John Studzinski
 Foundation
The Peggy Ramsay
 Foundation

SPONSORS
Barclays Bank plc
Bloomberg News
The Granada Group plc
Marks & Spencer plc
Business Members
American Airlines
AT&T (UK) Ltd
British Interactive
 Broadcasting Ltd
BSkyB
Channel Four Television
Chubb Insurance
 Company of Europe S.A.
Davis Polk & Wardwell
Deep End Design
Goldman Sachs
 International
Heidrick & Struggles
Lambie-Nairn
Lazard Brothers & Co. Ltd
Mishcon de Reya Solicitors
OgilvyOne
Redwood Publishing plc
Simons Muirhead & Burton
Sullivan & Cromwell
J Walter Thompson
Tomkins plc

PRIVATE SUBSCRIBERS
Patrons
Advanpress
Associated Newspapers Ltd
Citigate Communications
Chris Corbin
Greg Dyke
Homevale Ltd
Laporte plc
Lex Service plc
Barbara Minto
New Penny Productions Ltd
Noel Gay Organisation
A T Poeton & Son Ltd
Greville Poke
Sir George Russell
Richard Wilson

Benefactors
Bill Andrewes
Batia Asher
Elaine Attias
Larry & Davina Belling
Jeremy Bond
Katie Bradford
Julia Brodie
Julian Brookstone
Guy Chapman
Yuen-Wei Chew
Carole & Neville Conrad
Conway van Gelder
Coppard and Co.
Lisa Crawford Irwin
Curtis Brown Ltd
David Day
Robyn Durie
Winston Fletcher
Claire & William Frankel
Nicholas A Fraser
Norman Gerard

Henny Gestetner OBE
Carolyn Goldbart
Frank & Judy Grace
Sally Greene
Jan Harris
Angela Heylin
André Hoffman
Chris Hopson
Institute of Practitioners
 in Advertising
ICM Ltd
Peter Jones
Catherine Be Kemeny
Thomas & Nancy Kemeny
KPMG
Lady Lever
Collette & Peter Levy
Mae Modiano
Pat Morton
Sir Alan and Lady Moses
Joan Moynihan
Paul Oppenheimer
J C Orr
Sir Eric Parker
Carol Rayman
Angharad Rees
B J & Rosemary Reynolds
John Sandoe (Books) Ltd
Nicholas Selmes
David & Patricia Smalley
Max Stafford-Clark
Sue Stapely
Ann Marie Starr
Richard Turk
Elizabeth Tyson
Charlotte Watcyn Lewis

AMERICAN FRIENDS
Founders
Victoria Elenowitz
Monica Gerard-Sharp
Mia Martin Glickman
Dany Khosrovani
Mary Ellen Johnson
Benjamin Rauch
Rory Riggs
Robert Rosenkranz
Patrons
Miriam Bienstock
Richard and Linda Gelfond
Howard Gilman Foundation
Richard & Marcia Grand
Paul Hallingby
Carl Icahn & Gail Golden
Steven Magowan
William & Hilary Russell
Arielle Tepper
Benefactors
Mr and Mrs Mark Arnold
Harry Brown
Denise & Matthew Chapman
Abe & Florence Elenowitz
Brian & Araceli Keelan
Rudolph Rauch
Julie Talen
Members
Joanna Coles
Tom Hartman
Sharon King Hoge
Burt Lerner
Peter Lyden
Richard Medley & Maureen
 Murray
Douglas & Claudia Morse

FOR THE ROYAL COURT THEATRE

DIRECTION
Artistic Director	Ian Rickson
Director	Stephen Daldry
Assistant to the	
Artistic Director	Nicky Jones
Associate Directors	Elyse Dodgson
	James Macdonald*
	Max Stafford-Clark*
Trainee Director	Janette Smith **
Associate Director Casting	Lisa Makin
Casting Assistant	Julia Horan
Literary Manager	Graham Whybrow
Literary Assistant	Maja Jade
Literary Associate	Stephen Jeffreys*
Resident Dramatist	Rebecca Prichard+
International Administrator	Nathalie Bintener

PRODUCTION
Production Manager	Edwyn Wilson
Deputy Production Manager	Paul Handley
Head of Lighting	Johanna Town
Senior Electrician	Marion Mahon
Assistant Electricians	Michelle Green
	Maeve Laverty
Head of Stage	Martin Riley
Senior Carpenters	David Skelly
	Eddie King
	Terry Bennett
Head of Sound	Paul Arditti
Sound Deputy	Rich Walsh
Company Stage Manager	Cath Binks
Production Assistant	Sue Bird
Costume Deputies	Neil Gillies
	Rose Willis

YOUNG PEOPLE'S THEATRE
Associate Director	Ola Animashawun
General Manager	Aoife Mannix
Writers' Tutor	Noel Greig

ENGLISH STAGE COMPANY
President	Greville Poke
Vice President	Joan Plowright CBE
Council	
Chairman	Sir John Mortimer QC, CBE
Vice-Chairman	Anthony Burton
Members	Stuart Burge CBE
	Stephen Evans
	Sonia Melchett
	James Midgley
	Richard Pulford
	Nicholas Wright
	Alan Yentob
Advisory Council	Diana Bliss
	Tina Brown
	Allan Davis
	Elyse Dodgson
	Robert Fox
	Jocelyn Herbert
	Michael Hoffman
	Hanif Kureishi
	Jane Rayne
	Ruth Rogers
	James L. Tanner

MANAGEMENT
Executive Director	Vikki Heywood
Assistant to the	
Executive Director	Diana Pao
General Manager	Diane Borger
Finance Director	Donna Munday
Finance Officer	Rachel Harrison
Re-development	
Finance Officer	Neville Ayres
Finance & Administration	
Assistant	Eric Dupin

RE-DEVELOPMENT
Project Manager	Tony Hudson
Deputy Project Manager	Simon Harper
Assistant to Project Manager	Monica McCormack

MARKETING
Head of Marketing	Stuart Buchanan
Marketing Officer	Emily Smith
Press Officer	Giselle Glasman
Press for Toast	Sally Ann Lycett
	(for Guy Chapman Associates)
	tel: 01424 225140
Box Office Manager	Neil Grutchfield
Deputy Box Office Manager	Terry Cooke
Box Office Sales Operators	Glen Bowman
	Clare Christou
	Valli Dakshinamurthi
	Sophie Dart
	Jane Parker
	Carol Pritchard*
	Michele Rickett*
	Gregory Woodward

DEVELOPMENT
Development Director	Caroline Underwood
Assistant to	
Development Director	Ruth Gaucheron
Sponsorship Manager	Helen Salmon
Trusts and Foundations	Susan Davenport*
Development Assistant	Sophie Hussey
Fundraising Consultant	Joyce Hytner*

FRONT OF HOUSE
Acting Theatre Manager	Tim Brunsden
Deputy Theatre Manager	Sarah Harrison
Acting Deputy Theatre Manager	Jemma Davies
Duty House Manager	Gini Woodward*
Relief Duty House Managers	Neil Grutchfield*
	Marion Doherty*
	Lorraine Selby*
Bookshop Manager	Del Campbell
Bookshop Supervisor	Gini Woodward*
Maintenance	Greg Piggot*
Lunch Bar Caterer	Andrew Forrest*
Stage Door/Reception	Lorraine Benloss*
	Tyrone Lucas*
	Nettie Williams*
	Benjamin Till*
	Tom Hescott*
	Suzie Zara
Cleaners (Theatre Upstairs)	Maria Correia*
	Mila Hamovic*
	Peter Ramswell*
(Theatre Downstairs)	Avery Cleaning Services Ltd.
Firemen (Theatre Downstairs)	Myriad Security Services
(Theatre Upstairs)	Datem Fire Safety Services

Thanks to all of our bar staff and ushers
* part-time
\+ Arts Council Resident Dramatist
** This theatre has the support of the Harold Hyam Wingate Foundation under the Regional Theatre Young Director Scheme administered by Channel 4.

Royal Court Theatre
St. Martin's Lane, London, WC2E 4BG
Tel: 0171 565 5050 Fax: 0171 565 5001
Box Office: 0171 565 5000
www.royal-court.org.uk

First published in 1999 by Oberon Books Ltd.
(incorporating Absolute Classics),
521 Caledonian Road, London, N7 9RH
Tel: 0171 607 3637/ Fax: 0171 607 3629

British Library Cataloguing-in-Publication Data
A catalogue record for this book is available from the
British Library.

ISBN: 1 84002 104 7

Cover design and typography: Richard Doust
Front cover photograph: Adrian Fisk
Back cover photograph: Catherine Corr

Printed in Great Britain by MPG Books Limited, Cornwall

Author's Note

I would like to thank Jack Bradley (Royal National Theatre), Izzy Mant (Theatre Machine), Chris Campbell, Stephen Wright, Simon Tracy, Rose Cobbe, Pat Shaw, Andy Rashleigh, and Purni Morrell for reading the early drafts of the script, and for making intelligent suggestions during its proving.

I dedicate this play to Jo, my parents, and those people of Hull who, either by necessity or inspiration, found themselves involved in the mass production of bread during the seventies.

Scene 1

1975.

The smell of bread baking. The industrial thump, thump, thump of a bread plant oven drive.

The canteen of a bread factory. Stage right, along the wall, are various vending machines, and a hot water boiler over a sink with a mirror above. A health and safety notice board carries various notices and warnings, and has minutes of meetings stuck to it with drawing pins. An old joke notice, originally "YOU DON'T HAVE TO BE MAD TO WORK HERE – BUT IT HELPS!", has been defaced and now reads simply "HELP!" The original wording is crossed out but legible. There is a pay phone attached to the wall near the door. Next to that is a store cupboard. The floor is red industrial lino. From the door to the sink the floor is black with dirt and grease. A waste bin overflows with dead tea bags. The wall behind the bin is splattered with used tea bag hits and the floor about the bin has one or two tea bags which have missed their target. There is a partition running the whole length of the back wall. This partition is made up of two large glass windows either side of an opaque glass door. Through the stage right window we can see a flight of steel steps rising to the bread plant. Through the stage left window the steps descend to the ground floor, the offices and the locker room. Two large steel tables down stage are arranged lengthways, parallel to the vending machines. There is a large clock above the door – it shows ten to three. There is no way of knowing whether it is morning or afternoon. Similarly there is no clue as to the season.

ROBERT BLAKEY enters from the bread plant. He is wearing baker's whites, which have seen three or four shifts, and a striped office shirt with an open collar. He wears Buddy Holly style black spectacles. His hair is mid-seventies style with sideburns. His sleeves are rolled up. He is a physical man, prone to bouncing on his feet and touching his crotch unnecessarily. He has tattoos on each forearm. Slung over one shoulder is a holdall, over the other an acoustic guitar in a vinyl sleeve. He puts the holdall on the steel table nearest the sink and unzips it. The guitar he props against the table.

He takes out a mug, a tea bag, and a small jam jar with a screw top which contains milk. He puts the tea bag in the mug, walks to the boiler and fills it with hot water. He continues emptying out the contents of his holdall, marking his territory on the steel table. He goes over to a hook on the wall and takes a wooden clipboard from a nail and begins to study his work sheets, making calculations, and notes with a pencil. He then stands and goes to the phone. He dials and speaks.

BLAKEY: Mr Beckett? – it's me, Blakey... Oh, you know, mustn't grumble... ha! Nowt else to do on a Sunday is there... Na! This bakehouse is my church. Look, Frank's on holiday so I'm a man short, I'll have to do spare wank mesen. ... A student? I don't like students going on the ovens – their mothers complain... Aye, alright. ... Finish? Oh, early enough. One o'clock mebbe. Tarra. Oh, did you do my reference for Bradford?... Ta. ... Dunno what we'd do – our lass won't leave Hull. Might 'ave to come and live with your lot at South Cave eh!? Ha! I could join your golf club Mr Beckett! ... Ha, ha! Fucking right you wouldn't! Alright, tarra.

He puts the phone down.

(*Quietly.*) Cunt.

He takes his tea bag out of the mug, squeezes it, throws it at the bin and adds milk to his tea. He takes a sip. He takes his guitar out of the vinyl cover. After tuning the guitar incorrectly, he begins to play. He plays the first few bars badly and starts again. The second time he plays even worse.

Enter COLIN. BLAKEY, as if caught in an illicit act, abandons playing and makes as if tuning the guitar.

COLIN: How do Blakey?

BLAKEY: Colin.

18

COLIN is dressed in a blouson style leather jacket over baker's whites and a white baker's cap. He wears a white office shirt with short sleeves and a bakery workers' union tie. He also wears a long apron which makes it look a little like he's wearing a skirt. He puts his very large tupperware plastic lunch box on the table opposite BLAKEY and sits down.

COLIN: D'you hear Beckett's shagging that lass on custards?

BLAKEY: (*Without interest.*) Oh, aye.

COLIN: Yeah, the one with no teeth.

BLAKEY ignores him.

Bit young for 'aving no teeth – eh? Huh, has it's advantages though – eh?

BLAKEY shoots him a contemptuous glance. COLIN takes out a pen and a notebook. He checks the entries in one column and compares with another set of figures further in the book.

BLAKEY: What yer got there?

COLIN: Strike pay. You're due... two weeks on strike, ... married man, one child, ... three pound fifty.

He pushes it across to BLAKEY.

BLAKEY: What d'you get then?

COLIN: Four pound fifty. Two kids y'see.

BLAKEY: The strike was six weeks back. Three quid might 'ave been some use then.

BLAKEY takes the money.

COLIN: Give it back if you want. (*Beat.*) Who's spare wank tonight?

BLAKEY: Beckett's gor us a student.

COLIN: Oh fucking 'ell. I sat down with Beckett and we agreed we're not having no casual labour no more.

BLAKEY: I'm gonna put him on the ovens, which means you'll have to be spare.

COLIN: You're not listening are yer?

BLAKEY: No-one gives a flying fuck about that union of yours Colin. When you go up can you go on the ovens. I'm tekking Nellie off now. He's been going two hours without a break.

COLIN: He's been going forty fucking years without a break. (*Beat.*) What time tonight then?

BLAKEY: Easy. One mebbe.

COLIN: Nice.

COLIN looks at his watch and then the clock.

Eh, Blakey, if I tek Nellie off *now* will you do me a flier in't morning?

BLAKEY: Sorry, can't. Against the union agreement, on two counts. You're not supposed to mix...

COLIN: I've not supposed to have been mixing for three year.

BLAKEY: ... and no-one can have fliers, union rules.

COLIN: Oh! You're just bin bloody-minded now!

Pause.

BLAKEY: Alright, but don't tell no-one.

COLIN: Smashing! What's he on?

BLAKEY: Big 'olemeal next.

COLIN takes off his jacket and almost with enthusiasm skips towards the door. Opening it he meets CECIL coming in. CECIL is in his fifties, plump and grey-haired. He is immaculately dressed in full baker's whites and peaked cap. His whites are even ironed!

COLIN: How do Cecil?

CECIL: Colin. (*Looking at the clock.*) Eh? What's going on?

COLIN: Blakey's gonna do us a flier.

CECIL: Oh yes, very nice. I don't want a flier. I like it here.

COLIN continues up to the plant. CECIL enters. He puts his bag on the table. BLAKEY is dealing four hands of thirteen card brag.

You getting enough Blakey?

BLAKEY: A bit.

CECIL: Nice. Lovely.

PETER: (*Off.*) What the fuck are you doin' up there Colin? It's not three yet.

PETER can be seen through the stage left window ascending to the canteen.

COLIN: (*Off.*) Mind your own business.

Hearing PETER arriving CECIL tiptoes to the door and hides behind it. Enter PETER. PETER is young, with long, lank hair. His only protection against the filth and grease is a towel which he wears over fashionably flared trousers and a shirt with a round collar and pictures of galloping horses. As he passes CECIL, CECIL makes a successful grab for his balls, and squeezes them. PETER doubles up in pain.

21

PETER: Agghhhh! Fuck. Ohhh, fucking hell Cecil.

CECIL: One nil. Early in the shift. Promising start
– good early lead. See Colin's on mixing already.
Must have a bird up there. Blakey's gonna do him
a flier. What d'yer reckon to that Peter?

*PETER recovering, inspects a chair at the table for dirt before he
sits. He puts his bag on the table and empties the contents. PETER
has a frozen ready meal.*

PETER: I never get a fucking flier. Why's that
Blakey, eh?

BLAKEY: You can fuck off now if you want.

PETER: Aye, I might an' all.

CECIL: (*To BLAKEY.*) What's new?

BLAKEY: Beckett's shagging that lass on custards
– the one with no teeth.

CECIL: Lovely. I wouldn't say no to a custard
right now.

They pick up their cards and begin sorting.

PETER: What time tonight Blakey?

BLAKEY: Oneish.

CECIL: Oh, lovely!

*CECIL picks up his cards one by one. BLAKEY and PETER pick
up all thirteen at one go and sort them. Consequently CECIL reacts
to each new card.*

Got nowt here, oh no. Nothing, nowt, that's nice,
oh no, tragic.

PETER: (*To BLAKEY.*) We're a man short, aren't we?

CECIL: (*Referring to cards.*) What a steaming pile of shite!

BLAKEY: Yeah. (*Throwing his first hand down.*) One, two, three.

PETER: (*To CECIL, laying his cards.*) Yours. (*To BLAKEY.*) What if Dezzie don't show?

BLAKEY: Beckett's gor us a student.

CECIL: A student! Ho ho! Lovely! Marvellous. (*Laying cards.*) Three kings.

PETER: Well he ain't having my job.

BLAKEY: He's going with Dezzie.

CECIL: Mmmm, I wouldn't go with Dezzie. Oh no!

PETER: (*Knowingly.*) Is he here?

BLAKEY: Who? Dezzie?

PETER: Yeah.

CECIL: Mmm, too early for Dezzie.

Laying his third hand.

Two, three, four on the dog. Marvellous.

PETER: You wanna quarter the deckie bastard. It ain't fair on us. Ten minutes late every fucking shift.

BLAKEY: Dezzie never gets a flier.

PETER: Didn't even turn up Thursday and Friday. Good job we was on days.

CECIL: Jack flush.

The others throw their cards in and pay two pence to CECIL.

Very nice, thank you. Very kind of you. All square. Marvellous. Lovely. Oh yes.

PETER: Er... Blakey, look I'm gonna need a sub again. Can you ask Beckett for us?

CECIL: (*Getting his wallet out.*) Here, how much d'yer want son? Five quid, ten, fifteen?

PETER: Hundred and fifty.

CECIL: Oh bloody hell! Can't help with that, oh no, our lass would notice a hundred and fifty going out the back door, oh yes.

BLAKEY: I'll ask Beckett.

PETER: Ta.

NELLIE enters. He is a broken man of fifty-nine. He is wearing a string vest covered in brown dough. The dough is stuck to the vest. He wears brown leather shoes with no laces. He has a big, bony frame, built for endless physical labour. His speech is slow and slurred from fatigue. He carries a small package of greaseproof paper and an enamel mug with a string protected handle. He sits next to PETER. PETER takes a sideways look in disgust.

CECIL: How do Nellie?

NELLIE: Cecil.

PETER: (*To NELLIE.*) Eh, Nellie, did yer know someone's had a shit down your back?

NELLIE smiles, embarrassed, and unwraps his sandwiches.

You got new shoes, Nellie?

NELLIE: Yeah.

PETER: Where d'yer get them then?

NELLIE makes to talk but stops himself, looking at BLAKEY.

NELLIE: Someone.

PETER: Who?

NELLIE: (*NELLIE takes a look across at BLAKEY.*)
Dunno.

PETER: 'Kinell!

There is banging on the partition from above.

VOICE (*Shouting off.*) Come on! Oi! Let's be having
you! Three o'clock!

*All check the clock. It shows two minutes to three. PETER stands,
goes to the door, opens it and shouts up to the plant.*

PETER: You're not getting a flier out of me,
Les Jackson!

He shuts the door and returns to the table.

(*To CECIL.*) Never gives me a flier.

CECIL: What's your lass done for you tonight,
Nellie?

NELLIE: (*Embarrassed/quiet.*) Cheese.

PETER: What was that Nellie?

NELLIE: (*A bit louder.*) Cheese.

CECIL: Mmm, lovely, cheese, mm. Marvellous.

PETER: (*Confrontationally at NELLIE.*) You work
eighty hours a fucking week and she gives you
fucking cheese.

CECIL: Oh I like cheese.

PETER: Not every fucking night you don't.

BLAKEY: What you mixing, Nellie?

PETER picks a piece of dough from NELLIE's vest.

PETER: Don't tell me! Brown.

CECIL: Ho, ho, ho! I don't like brown myself. Do you like a bit of brown Blakey?

BLAKEY: For a change.

CECIL: Oh, right, lovely. I understand. Very nice. Wouldn't touch it myself.

BLAKEY: (*To NELLIE.*) Big uns or little uns?

NELLIE: Farmhouse.

PETER: Fucking farmer brown. Why do they call it farmhouse?

CECIL: Looks like a farmhouse, oh yes.

PETER: How can a loaf of bread look like a fucking farmhouse?

CECIL: Imagination. (*He shuts his eyes.*) Chickens, oh yes, sheepdog, pond, ducks. Mmmm. Yes.

PETER: Poxy loaf of fucking bread.

CECIL: ... and two horses... shagging.

Banging on the partition.

VOICE: (*Shouting off.*) Come on yer lazy bastards!

BLAKEY: Alright – let's be having you – it's three.

PETER: Er... Blakey, my old china, my special mucker, how about one man on the ovens, just to start like.

BLAKEY: Cecil?

CECIL: Mmm. Peak of fitness. Early in the shift. Very keen.

BLAKEY gives the nod. PETER and CECIL stand and leave. NELLIE stands, wearily, and walks over to the boiler and fills his mug. He sits and takes a cigarette from a new packet of twenty in his top pocket. He looks at his cheese sandwiches and wraps them again. He covets PETER's meal.

BLAKEY: Shoes alright?

NELLIE: Couldn't find no laces.

BLAKEY: I got some spare uns downstairs.

DEZZIE enters in a desperate rush. He is a small, wiry man and under his motorcycle helmet there is a classic D.A. haircut. His fingers and arms have faded blue tattoos – typical of trawler deckhands – anchors, Mom & Dad etc. He takes a look at the clock which is showing past three. He catches BLAKEY's imperious glare. In a rush he puts his snap tin on the second table. He tries to undo the straps on his motorbike helmet but struggles with them. He looks at the clock again. He considers going up on the plant with his helmet on, decides against it, and struggles a bit longer with the helmet.

DEZZIE: Bloody hell!

He eventually decides to go up wearing the helmet and exits. Almost immediately he comes back through the door with his helmet in his hand. He puts it on the table, looks at BLAKEY, looks at the clock again.

Shit!

BLAKEY: Sit down Dezzie. Cecil's doing the oven on his tod.

(Preparing to write.) You got your new address?

DEZZIE: Aye, right. (*He thinks fiercely.*)

Pause.

No. I've forgotten it. Sorry. It's Orchard Park somewhere.

BLAKEY: Phone number?

DEZZIE: (*Searching his pockets.*) I've got the number... somewhere. Our lass wrote it down.

BLAKEY: (*Referring to writing on the helmet.*) Is this it?

DEZZIE: Aye, yeah. That's it.

BLAKEY: (*Copying it down.*) Wor 'appened Thursday then?

DEZZIE: Check up – for the snip. I've gorra go back next Wednesday. Yeah, they wanted a sample.

BLAKEY: What – you couldn't get it up?

DEZZIE: No, but, Thursday, was my mother's birthday.

BLAKEY: So?

DEZZIE: Well, I never wank on my mother's birthday. (*To NELLIE.*) You don't wank on your mother's birthday, do you Nellie?

NELLIE: (*Matter of factly.*) No.

BLAKEY: Beckett's none too chuffed.

DEZZIE: Did he say owt?

BLAKEY: Na, blames himself for giving a deckie a job. Can you take Peter off? He's tinning up.

DEZZIE: Aye. Er... ta.

He exits to the bread plant.

BLAKEY: Dezzie.

NELLIE: Aye, Dezzie.

Enter LANCE. He is mid-thirties. He wears country tweeds and leather brogues, and a red rugby shirt with white collar. He carries a brown leather briefcase. His hair is collar-length and unkempt. He carries a letter in a buff envelope.

LANCE: Good afternoon. I'm looking for Mr Blakey. I presume he's the manager. I'm to start work on the bread plant at three.

BLAKEY, knowing it's later, glances at the clock.

Ah! Yes, yes. sorry.

BLAKEY: You won't find owt in the way of management here on a Sunday.

LANCE: Yes... right! Er... well... er...

BLAKEY stands and walks around LANCE inspecting him.

BLAKEY: D'you support Arsenal?

LANCE: It's a rugby shirt.

BLAKEY: No ball games on the bread plant.

LANCE: This is the bread plant then?

BLAKEY: Are you the student?

LANCE: Yes. Lance Bishop.

BLAKEY: You ever had crabs?

LANCE: No.

BLAKEY: I have – twice. (*Beat.*) Bishop eh? Busy day for you then – Sunday.

LANCE: Agnostic actually.

BLAKEY: You ever worked for a living?

LANCE: Yes, yes. But not er... factory work.

BLAKEY: (*Offering his hand.*) Blakey, Robert Blakey. This is Walter Nelson. Our mixer.

BLAKEY and LANCE shake hands. LANCE offers his hand to NELLIE, but NELLIE doesn't take it up, although there is no thinking behind the refusal.

LANCE: Walter. Pleased to meet you.

NELLIE: How do?

BLAKEY: We work a six-day week. Nights is three till finish. Finish can be anywhere between eleven at night to three in't morning. Wednesdays and Thursdays we work a twelve-hour shift – seven at night till seven in't morning. Last day is Friday – three till finish again. That's a sixteen-hour day on Friday, and maybe a few hours of Saturday morning thrown in. Then you're back here again Sunday morning at seven. How's that grab yer?

LANCE: Is that legal?

BLAKEY: You get paid. Bit old for a student aren't you?

LANCE: I'm a mature student actually. Social and economic history.

BLAKEY: History's bunk innit?

LANCE: Ah, yes, very good. But er... "more or less bunk" was what he actually said.

BLAKEY: Henry Ford.

LANCE: He'd like it here.

BLAKEY: No he wouldn't. Let me see your hands.

LANCE is reticent. He holds back.

I gorra check for dermatitis.

LANCE puts his bag down and holds out his hands, palms down. BLAKEY takes his hands and turns them palms up. BLAKEY, seeing LANCE's scarred left wrist, pushes up LANCE's cuff for a better look at his wound. LANCE is embarrassed.

If I were you I'd keep them cuffs rolled down like you had 'em. Our oven won't bite so hard that way.

BLAKEY goes to a cupboard and takes out two pairs of coarse sackcloth oven gloves, which he gives to LANCE.

Wear two pair of gloves. Last student we had lasted two hours. Burnt to fuck he was. I had to tek him to infirmary mesen. Crying he was. Sociologist. Come with me, Sir Lancelot. I'm gonna put you on the oven. You ever seen a reel oven?

LANCE: Well, I think I've seen one but...

BLAKEY: It's not dangerous so long as you keep up with it, and don't panic when it gets ahead.

The phone rings. BLAKEY answers it. LANCE reads the notices.

(*On the phone.*) Bread plant... Yeah, it's me... Hello Mr Beckett, what's up... You wanna come in and do a shift?... Ha, ha! I'd treat yer well... Mmm... Mm... You what?... Are you pulling my plonker? ... Fuck... How many?... Oh for fuck's sake! ... That'll tek us till four in morning. How many again? ... Wi' lids? ... Right... Well, you could've told 'em to fuck off... Yeah, yeah, yeah, yeah...

I know, if Bradford ses bek it we gorra bek it...
They'll send an artic yeah?... Right, tarra.

He puts the phone down.

Cunt!

NELLIE: Summat wrong?

BLAKEY: Skeltons 'ave 'ad a fuck-up. Bradford are
telling us to do three thousand for 'em.

NELLIE: Big uns?

BLAKEY: Aye. (*To LANCE.*) Huh, you're gonna 'ave
some fun tonight sunshine. So, Walter, what's this?

NELLIE: Smoke.

BLAKEY: Right, I'll get Colin to switch to big
stuff straight off and we'll split the wholemeal
into two runs.

NELLIE: What time's finish then?

BLAKEY: Well, by rights now it's gonna be four in
morning but I'll be fucked if I'm gonna 'ang
around. I'll knock the oven back to twenny-five,
and we'll leg it all night.

NELLIE: Aye.

BLAKEY: Come on Sir Lancelot.

*LANCE and BLAKEY exit to the bread plant. NELLIE, alone,
takes out a cigarette from his packet of twenty. He looks at the clock,
thinks and puts it back. He takes out one of his cheese sandwiches,
separates the bread from the cheese, throws the bread away and eats
the cheese. He just sits. Occasionally he will rub his head or his nose
and flick any hard bits of dough he finds off his fingers. His head
hangs. Enter PETER. He bursts energetically and angrily through
the door.*

PETER: Have you heard the fucking news Walte

NELLIE: Yeah.

PETER: Three thousand for fucking Skellies!
 Why can't they bek their own bread? We'll be
 doing ten hours of big stuff! Bill and Ben the
 slicing men won't get to go home at all! (*Beat.*)
 Don't bother you though does it? Ah, fuck. You
 alright Walter?

NELLIE: Yeah. You on a smoke?

PETER checks a chair for dirt, brushes the seat and sits.

PETER: Ha! Yeah, that's the way it works innit.
 You ger a smoke before you've even started and
 you can't get one later on when you're on big
 stuff. Who's that then?

NELLIE: Student.

PETER: Student? Fucking Lord Muck more like.

NELLIE: Who's mixing?

PETER: Must be down to the bones of his bum if
 he's working here.

NELLIE: Is Colin mixing?

PETER: I couldn't give a monkey's toss who's
 mixing Walter. Neither should you. You're on
 your break. Have a fucking break pal. 'Kinnel!

NELLIE: Must be Colin.

PETER: You wanna watch that Colin you know.
 He's after your job. Either that or chargehand.
 (*Beat.*) You retire soon don't yer?

NELLIE: Na.

33

PETER: How long you got then?

NELLIE: Six year.

PETER: You gor owt lined up?

NELLIE: Na.

PETER: Got your caravan, ain't yer?

NELLIE: Yeah.

PETER: Are you going there this summer?

NELLIE: Yeah.

PETER: Bet it's nice eh? Sea air, grass, sand. Sea, air – caravan. (*Beat.*) Wouldn't catch me in a fucking caravan.

NELLIE: Aye.

PETER: No fucking Beckett telling you what to do. Are you going on yer tod or wi' your lass?

NELLIE: Yeah.

PETER: You and the missus, eh? What do you do then? Fish?

NELLIE: Na.

PETER: What – walk? Swim?

NELLIE: Na.

PETER: Where's the caravan? Is it on one of them big sites – you know bingo, disco, shops, an evening with the Troggs?

NELLIE: Na.

PETER: It's not!? Right, glad we got that sorted out. Where is it then?

NELLIE: Field.

PETER: What sort of field?

NELLIE: (*Under pressure.*) Field.

PETER: Yeah, you told me that. What sort of field?

NELLIE: Farmer's field.

PETER: Nice! Good! A farmer's field. So what you gonna do then? In this farmer's field.

NELLIE: Dunno.

PETER: No?

NELLIE: No.

PETER: I can see you Walter, rolling around in't grass with your lass. Mekking daisy chains!

NELLIE: Yeah.

PETER: You put your feet up Walter. Fuck me, you've earned it.

NELLIE: Aye.

Silence.

PETER: Are you having a holiday Peter? Well, thanks for asking Walter. As a matter o' fact our lass is dead keen on going to Crete for a couple of weeks, though I reckon we'll end up at her mother's again, but thanks very much for your interest all the same Walter.

NELLIE rubs his face embarrassed.

NELLIE: Germans i'nt there?

PETER: Crete? Fucking tanks everywhere Walter. They don't bother me. I'd share a tent with

Hermann Goering and give him a blow job every night just to ger away from this shit hole.

Seeing COLIN coming down the steps.

Wouldn't have to clap eyes on that cunt Colin neither.

Enter COLIN.

How do Colin?!

COLIN: Peter. Nellie.

NELLIE: How do?

COLIN begins opening his tupperware boxes. One is a mug, one contains the tea, another the milk, yet another the sugar etc.

COLIN: D'you hear Beckett's shagging that lass from custards. The one with no teeth.

PETER: What? She's got no teeth at all?

COLIN: Na. She's got false teeth.

PETER: So she's got some teeth then.

COLIN: Yeah, but they're not her own.

PETER: Who's fucking teeth are they then?

COLIN: You know what I mean.

PETER: I don't know what the fuck you're on about. Mekking up a load of crap about some lass who goes around borrowing teeth. (*Beat.*) You're shop steward – mek yoursen useful will yer – ring Beckett and tell him to stick his Skeltons' order up his arse... please.

Pause.

COLIN: What's new Nellie?

PETER: Walter 'ere's going on holiday.

COLIN: Your caravan?

NELLIE: Aye.

COLIN: Picking tatties again?

PETER: Oh, 'kinnel! For fuck's sake Walter give yourself a proper holiday. Picking fucking tatties! Please!

COLIN: He enjoys it. Don't you Nellie?

PETER: Oh fuck off!

COLIN: Even if you didn't your lass would mek you – wouldn't she? Ain't that right Nellie?

PETER: His name's Walter.

COLIN: It would do you good Peter.

PETER: You what?

COLIN: Hardly work, what you do, is it? Tinning up. Rubbing your nob against a greasy bar all night. Some people'd pay to have a go on there.

PETER: You bin lairy?

COLIN: Just saying. Bit of hard graft might suit you. You know what they say – a change is as good as a rest. Cards?

PETER: Na. (*Beat.*) Picking tatties. Walter, Walter, fucking Walter!

PETER stands and washes out his tea cup.

COLIN: What's your lass done for you tonight, Nellie?

NELLIE: Cheese.

COLIN: Ooh! Very nice.

NELLIE: What you on?

COLIN: I've just mixed a run of big 'olemeal.

NELLIE: Blakey tek you off?

COLIN: Aye. He's dumped the student with Dezzie on the ovens.

NELLIE: Cecil changing tins yet?

PETER: Give it a rest will yer Walter?! Yer on a smoke! Read the fucking paper, do the crossword, go to sleep, eat, drink, smoke, fucking fuck! The bread plant's a million miles up them steps, and you're in here for the purpose of rest and recreation, refuelling, meditation, cogitation and fucking elevation!

He sits.

Here have a ciggie. I'll talk to you. Let's discuss the issues of the day.

He gives him a cigarette and lights it for him.

Off you go. Go on, you start – I'll jump on board once you're up and running. Fire away! Politics – Ted Heath, eh? What d'yer reckon? Is he a puff? Eh? (*Beat.*) Alright let's try football. Leeds, eh? Don Revie – footballing genius, unlucky bastard, or puff – what d'yer reckon?

COLIN: Change the record.

PETER: What about Colin, here? Eh? What d'yer

reckon, eh? Good mixer, committed shop steward, eh, or puff? Eh, what do you reckon?

COLIN squirms. NELLIE rubs his face in embarrassment.

(*To himself.*) You lot wind me up.

PETER draws a cigarette for himself and then puts his packet away. COLIN not having been offered one, takes out his own packet draws one and lights it. NELLIE wraps up his cheese sandwiches, pushes back his chair, and stands.

COLIN: (*To NELLIE, checking his watch.*) What was that Nellie – smoke or half hour?

NELLIE: Smoke.

Exit NELLIE to bread plant. PETER and COLIN are left alone. COLIN, self-consciously, fiddles with his tupperware boxes. PETER watches with contempt.

COLIN: Sold that car of yours yet?

PETER: No. Why?

COLIN: What do you want for it?

PETER: Hundred. Hundred and fifty to you.

COLIN: (*Knowing he's not.*) You gerrin a better one then?

Pause.

PETER ignores him, stands and inspects the vending machine – looking for a cool drink. Enter CECIL from the bread plant, chirpy and full of energy. He breezes in, and seeing PETER bending down to pick out his can from the vending machine tray, grabs his balls from behind and squeezes them hard. PETER doubles up in very genuine pain.

PETER: (*Swearing quietly.*) Oh fffffuck. Oh!

CECIL: Two nil. Marvellous. Two up already, not even dark yet.

PETER: Oh God that hurts.

CECIL takes out his mug and prepares a cup of tea.

CECIL: You heard about this Skellies' order, Colin?

COLIN: Course.

CECIL: Oh yes, Blakey's going spare up there. Ho, ho! Chucking tins about, oh yes. Not a happy man. Me, I love it here, oh yes. You getting enough Colin?

COLIN: No complaints.

CECIL: I'm not getting any.

COLIN: You go fishing yesterday?

CECIL: Oh yes. Up Wansford beck. Lovely. Marvellous day. Perfect.

COLIN: D'yer catch owt?

CECIL: Oh no, nothing. (*Beat.*) Student's had a go at himself. Seen his wrists? Serious.

PETER: What suicide?

CECIL: Oh yes, unsuccessful attempt I should think.

PETER: He'll wish he were dead when lids start going on.

CECIL: That oven'll tek off in a minute Blakey's got it going that fast. Oh yes.

COLIN: Oh aye, what speed?

CECIL: About thirty.

COLIN: He'll fucking blow us all up will Blakey. Hardly new plant this place is it?

CECIL: Skeltons is all new plant. Look at them. Yes. Like the Germans.

PETER: You what?

CECIL: Superior technology, inferior manpower. Oh, yes.

PETER: Best thing that ever happened to you – that war.

CECIL: It's the only thing that's ever happened to me. Oh yes. Marvellous time.

DEZZIE: (*Off.*) ALL YER DANISH!

CECIL: That's the Danish off. Could do with a nice bit o' Danish.

COLIN: Blakey took that last student to hospital at two in't morning.

CECIL: Nice lad. Useless, but nice. Sociologist. Oh yes.

PETER: They don't pay no tax you know. He'll take home more than me this week.

CECIL: I don't mind. What do I need money for? Do this for love. Only loving I'm getting. Least I see more of my money than Nellie does. Oh yes.

PETER: How's that?

CECIL: Takes his wage packet home sealed up – his lass opens it. Oh yes.

COLIN: (*To PETER.*) Same as you then, Peter.

PETER: I got three bairns to feed. (*To CECIL.*)
 Where's Nellie get his smokes then?

CECIL: She gis him one packet of twenny on
 a Satdy morning and that lasts him all week.
 Three a day.

PETER: That's twenny-one.

COLIN: Yeah, that's why if you see Nellie at back
 end of Friday's shift he's always gagging for
 a smoke.

PETER: No point trying to cadge one off him then?

CECIL: Mm, he's got them numbered in there.
 Oh yes.

PETER: I wouldn't let no woman get the better of
 me like that.

CECIL: He met her here he did. She worked
 downstairs, she did. Oh yes.

COLIN: What was she on?

PETER: Cheese sarnies!

They laugh.

CECIL: Eccles cakes. Many years ago. Oh yes.
 Whirlwind romance I understand. Wonderful
 woman. I've never met her.

COLIN: There's a photograph of the wedding in
 Beckett's office. Nellie looks very smart, top hat
 an' all.

PETER: I bet he was back here for the night shift.

CECIL: Oh yes, must've been.

COLIN pulls out his union book.

COLIN: Oh, er... strike money. I haven't paid you yet have I.

PETER: Strike! Strike was months ago. Some fucking union we've got. Management offer us thirty-six quid, thirty-*six*, it was there on the fucking table! But oh no, union goes on strike for forty pound; and we're back at work for thirty-*three* quid. Management are fucking laughing at us.

CECIL: Oh yes, terrible strike. You couldn't get bread anywhere. Upset our lass it did. We drove to Bridlington one day, you know, to have a look around – didn't find much. Couple of baps, that's all, and they were stale. Oh yes.

COLIN: Five pound then, Peter.

PETER: Ta.

There is banging against the partition. DEZZIE's head comes into view. PETER and COLIN look at the clock. DEZZIE rushes back to the oven.

DEZZIE: (*Off.*) Oi! Peter! Let's be having you!

COLIN: You on smokes or half hours Peter?

PETER: Fuck off.

COLIN: Just you and your lass, Cecil?

CECIL: Oh yes, me and the missus. No-one else. Her and me, just the two of us, on us tod.

COLIN: Two pounds.

CECIL: Lovely, very generous. Thank you. All understood.

Enter BLAKEY hot and flustered.

PETER: Eh, Blakey what's this about Skeltons?

BLAKEY: They've had a fuck-up. Bradford's told us to mek up for them.

PETER: Fuck Bradford, this is Hull!

COLIN: What time tonight then?

BLAKEY: Three thirty. Mebbe.

COLIN: Beckett must think we all just come down in the last shower.

BLAKEY: That's what I told him when he rang. I said "You must think we all just come down in the last shower Mr Beckett. We're not fucking doing it – it's a Sunday."

COLIN: You said that to Beckett?

BLAKEY: On the phone – just now. He had to get Bradford to ring and threaten us.

COLIN: Who at Bradford?

BLAKEY: Calvert.

COLIN: Beckett rang Calvert, on a Sunday, to get him to ring you?

BLAKEY: Aye, from his golf club.

COLIN: Beckett rang Calvert on a Sunday, at his golf club, to get him to ring you, here, in Hull?

BLAKEY: I know. You'd think I were mekking it up, wouldn't yer.

COLIN: What we doin for 'em then?

BLAKEY: Eighteen hundred twenty-eight ounce and twelve hundred tins – sliced.

COLIN: So, what – eighteen hundred or three thousand?

BLAKEY: I said! Three thousand!

COLIN: Alright!

Pause.

CECIL: Three thirty, lovely.

BLAKEY: Three mebbe.

PETER: It's coming down all the time.

BLAKEY: I got me ways.

PETER: Eh, Blakey – I don't want you fucking about with that oven, I've got to put my dinner in there later on.

BLAKEY: When you gonna eat it?

PETER: Eh? My half hour.

BLAKEY: You've had your half, and you're not getting another. You've chosen a bad night to tek the piss Peter.

PETER: I were going back now!

BLAKEY: I don't want you to. Dezzie's doing the oven on 'is tod. It's only 'olemeal. The student's on tinning up.

COLIN is smirking openly.

PETER: Fuck. (*To COLIN.*) What are you laughing at?

CECIL has picked up the ready meal and is inspecting it.

CECIL: (*Reading.*) "Chicken Kiev." Oh yes!

PETER: You're not getting none of it, Cecil.

CECIL: And I was going to offer you one of my fish paste rolls. Oh yes, every intention.

PETER: Fish paste! I wouldn't eat that shit if I were starving. You wanna live a bit! We've got an oven going all night. You could cook owt yer like in there.

COLIN: (*Grabbing the meal out of CECIL's hand.*) Let me see that. "Forty-five minutes on Gas mark 5." Our oven's no use to you then Peter. Blakey'll have ours down to twenny-five soon enough.

PETER: Twenty-five! I'd like to see that student doing big stuff with lids at that speed. If a lid comes off...

BLAKEY: No lids are gonna be coming off.

COLIN: Yebsley had his accident when we was rushing. The oven was only on thirty then.

BLAKEY: Yebsley's an headcase. He had it coming.

PETER: What did he do – Yebsley?

COLIN: Got his arm crushed.

PETER: I know that, but *how* did he do it?

COLIN: (*Illustrating with his arms.*) He got one tray behind putting lids on, so he reached into the oven chasing the rising tray. The empty tray trapped the arm he was reaching in with against the oven side, and the oven, been the bastard that it is, just kept going.

PETER: Oh fucking hell! Shut up!

CECIL: He's given up singing since then too. Terrible shame. Had a lovely voice. Used to sing on nights he did. "Open the door Richard, open the door and let me in." Played Stevadores and Dockers club once – got paid. Oh yes.

COLIN: Played guitar properly an' all.

BLAKEY: Colin. Give Dezzie a smoke will you.

COLIN: But Peter were...

BLAKEY: I told you! This is his half hour. When half hours come round he gets ten minutes.

COLIN: Right! Dezzie eh?

COLIN packs his tupperware box and leaves, taking the box with him onto the plant. The door shuts.

PETER: Fucking queer.

CECIL: Got a missus and two kids. Mind you so did Baden-Powell. Oh yes.

BLAKEY: Three kids actually. Two girls and a boy.

PETER: What – Colin?

BLAKEY: No Baden-Powell.

PETER: How do you know?

BLAKEY: I read a book.

PETER: Why? Were it the only book in prison?

CECIL: (*Quickly grabbing his arm.*) Eh, now Peter, come on. No need for that.

PETER: I just wanna know why.

CECIL: Interesting man, military hero – Mafeking and all that. Oh yes.

PETER: Maffefuckinwhat?

CECIL: Mafeking. He was at Mafeking.

PETER: Who was?

BLAKEY: Fucking Colin! Who do you think!?

PETER: You two 'ave been here over long. Oven's baked your brains. I won't be here for another Christmas. I'm not gonna end up talking bollocks.

CECIL: Bollocks, bollocks – bollocks, bollocks. Oh yes, bollocks.

Enter DEZZIE. He goes to the sink and washes his hands.

BLAKEY: That student alright Dezzie?

DEZZIE: Lance, aye. He could talk the hind legs off a donkey.

CECIL: Met your match then!

PETER: You moved house yet Dez?

DEZZIE: Last Wednesday. Yeah, it's grand. Hot water. Turn of the tap. Just like this. Beautiful.

PETER: Course, you had fuck all down Strickie Ave, didn't yer?

BLAKEY stands and exits to the plant.

DEZZIE: Yeah. We both had baths last night. Well, all of us. Got the kids off fost, then I had one, and then our lass had a go. I waited for her in't bedroom. Kaw! When she come in it were like a movie.

CECIL: Little towel eh? Mmm very nice. Was it good? Eh?

DEZZIE: Smashing.

PETER: What yer got? Gas?

DEZZIE: Eh?

PETER: How d'yer heat yer water?

DEZZIE: I dunno. Where do you look?

CECIL: Ho ho! Where do you look. Yes, very good.

DEZZIE offers his cigarettes around. CECIL declines, PETER accepts.

PETER: Well if it's gas you'll have a boiler in the kitchen. Oil, you might have outside. If it's lekky it'll be an immersion tank at top of stairs.

DEZZIE: I dunno.

CECIL: Are you on a promise tonight Dez?

DEZZIE: Oh aye! I can't tell you it's like she's a different woman.

CECIL: Lovely.

DEZZIE: Cos she's all clean like, I don't mind doing a bit of what she likes. Give the little man in a boat some attention, you with me?

CECIL: Oh yes. Row, row, row the boat.

BLAKEY bangs on the window, aggressively indicating that PETER's half hour is over. PETER stands immediately.

DEZZIE: What's up with him tonight?

PETER: What? You not heard? Skeltons 'ave 'ad a fuck-up. We're doing three thousand big uns for 'em.

DEZZIE: No, you're winding me up. You're just saying that cos I'm on a promise.

PETER exits to the plant laughing.

He's pulling me plonker ain't he?

CECIL: Unfortunately not Dez. Beckett rang through 'bout ten minutes back.

DEZZIE: Oh no! I'll have to ring our lass. Save her getting all spruced up for nowt.

CECIL: How long's it tek you to get home?

DEZZIE: About ten minutes. Have you got five p?

CECIL gives him a five pence piece.

CECIL: Are you on the bike?

DEZZIE: Motorbike, yeah.

CECIL: Go on your half hour then. Ten minutes there, ten minutes back – that'd give you ten minutes. Lovely.

DEZZIE: It teks me ten minutes to get me helmet off.

DEZZIE stands and moves to the phone.

CECIL: Well don't tek your helmet off then. Kinky. Very nice.

DEZZIE: (*On the phone.*) Nance? It's me... Yeah, Skeltons' plant is buggered or summat. We'll be here till... what time Cecil?

CECIL: Four.

DEZZIE: (*On the phone.*) – four... Yeah, I know. Me too. Is the water hot again tonight? ... Smashin'! What time are you gonna bed then love? ... Twelve. Aye. Don't wait up then. Yeah, I know. Bye love... Tomorrow? Mebbe, aye, we'll see. Bye.

He puts the phone down.

CECIL: On for tomorrow eh?

DEZZIE: Mebbe.

CECIL: Lovely. (*Beat.*) Are you going to decorate then?

DEZZIE: Gonna do it all pistachio.

CECIL: Oh lovely. (*Beat.*) What colour is that then?

DEZZIE: I dunno. I told her she can do it any colour she likes as long as it's not green.

CECIL: Our lass is very good around the house. Likes everything clean she does. But I'm not getting much.

DEZZIE: Why's that then?

CECIL: Dunno. She used to be interested. Never what you'd call keen, but interested, occasionally. But not now.

DEZZIE: Have you got hot water?

CECIL: Oh yes. It's not that.

DEZZIE: You're hardly newlyweds are you, I wouldn't worry about it.

CECIL: Oh I'm not asking for much. Just a bit to keep me going. When I'm on days.

DEZZIE: What can I say Cecil? (*Beat.*) Do you want a cup of tea?

CECIL: No, no you don't have to say owt. She's happy. Got the garden how she likes it.

DEZZIE: She likes gardening does she?

CECIL: Oh no, no. She's had it paved over. That's what she wanted. Did it mesen. Oh yes. Get it level. That's the trick.

DEZZIE: Is that easy then?

CECIL: Oh no. Virtually impossible.

DEZZIE: Eh, is it true Cecil, in Hull you're allowed to bury at least one person in your back garden?

CECIL: Ha! Who told you that?

DEZZIE: Blakey.

CECIL: Taking the Michael there I believe. Oh yes.

DEZZIE: Blakey said Hull were different from rest of country – you know like with the white phone boxes, and that.

CECIL: Well, you've been at sea all your life haven't you, Dez. You get Blakey on a trawler, and he wouldn't know what was going on would he.

BLAKEY enters. Goes straight for his mug and tea bags. He carries a pair of sackcloth oven gloves which he puts on the table.

DEZZIE: Where have you come from?

BLAKEY: Tin change.

DEZZIE: I thought you were on the ovens.

BLAKEY: Colin's taken over. The student hasn't had a smoke yet.

CECIL: I'll tek him off. No problem.

BLAKEY: Big 'olemeal with lids.

CECIL: Oh very nice!

CECIL stands and sorts his bag.

DEZZIE: Is Lance doing lids yet?

BLAKEY: Yeah. He's alright.

DEZZIE: (*Surprised.*) What? He's doing both his lids, *and* both his tins?

BLAKEY: Yeah. (*Beat.*) He's gerrin burnt but it don't seem to bother him.

CECIL: Right, lids, ho, ho, lovely.

CECIL exits to the plant.

DEZZIE: Skeltons eh?

BLAKEY: Aye.

DEZZIE: Running fast then eh?

BLAKEY: We can go faster.

DEZZIE: You starting half hours early?

BLAKEY: When I take Nellie off. Why?

DEZZIE: Nothing. Don't matter to me. Can't do nowt in half hour can yer?

BLAKEY: No you can't.

BLAKEY makes himself a cup of tea. He looks worried, fretful. He looks at his jobsheets. Stirs his tea.

DEZZIE: Will Bradford close us down, like they say?

BLAKEY: Yeah. When we cock up. Until then this place is easy money for them. No management, no investment, no maintenance, nowt really.

DEZZIE: But why make bread in Bradford for Hull, when we can mek it here, in Hull?

COLIN: They've poured money into new plant so they want a return.

DEZZIE: Yeah, but it...

BLAKEY: Look, if you've just bought a new car you're not gonna keep the old one just cos it still goes are you?

DEZZIE: Aye I reckon. What's the point of rushing though. I mean, you'll only save half hour.

BLAKEY: Yeah. I'm never in a good mood working on a Sunday, cos I spend all week looking forward to the weekend and then when the weekend comes I realise I work weekends, well Sundays.

DEZZIE: Yeah, I can't get used to working here neither. It's living at home. When I were on trawlers I always felt, you know, special in my own home, like a guest. I don't feel nowt special no more.

BLAKEY: Hero of the cod wars returns to Strickie Ave.

DEZZIE: Yeah, as a deckie, I felt like I were

someone, I were me, Dezzie. I mean, I'm still me. I'm *me*! Are you wimme? But... I dunno. Do you know what I'm saying? You've read a bit, ain't yer. You know what I'm on about. I'm still me, but working here, I'm not the same 'me', what I was before when I were a deckie.

BLAKEY: Identity. Working on trawlers is a clear identity. You're a deckie.

DEZZIE: Identity. Aye, that's it. It's a bugger, ain't it?

BLAKEY: Clear identity as a deckie – work hard, play hard, crap haircut.

DEZZIE: (*Slightly unsure.*) Yeah. Our lass likes it though. She can wave me off now. Weren't allowed to do that when I were fishing. Bad luck innit. Never stopped her though. She always used to wave and I'd go "Stop fucking waving will yer!"

BLAKEY: What's wrong with waving?

DEZZIE: Unlucky ain't it. And she'd say "I just want to say goodbye", and I'd say "Don't say goodbye!"

BLAKEY: What's wrong with "goodbye"?

DEZZIE: Unlucky!

BLAKEY: Course.

DEZZIE: And then she'd start crying, blubbing away like it were going out of fashion, and I'd say "Stop *crying* will yer!"

BLAKEY: Unlucky is it – crying?

DEZZIE: Na. It's just fucking hard work ain't it. But she don't wave, or say goodbye now.

Don't cry neither. Huh, not gonna die here
am I?

BLAKEY: Dunno. Yebsley nearly did.

DEZZIE: Aye. What do you think'd 'appen to
Nellie? You, know, if Bradford closed us.

BLAKEY: Drop dead.

DEZZIE: You reckon?

BLAKEY: He's worked here, what, forty, forty-five
year? He started at fourteen – delivering bread
on a box bike.

DEZZIE: To Bradford probably.

BLAKEY: Him and the oven have got a lot in
common. Industrial engineer from Bradford
'ad a look at our oven once and told Beckett
never to turn it off, never let it cool down.
Said it'd seize up. Could've been talking
about Nellie.

DEZZIE: What would you do?

BLAKEY: Our lass is working. Wouldn't mind
spending some time with my guitar. See a bit
more of my lad. Dunno.

DEZZIE: You'd be crawling up the walls after a week.

BLAKEY: At least they'd be my fucking walls.

BLAKEY stands and prepares to go back on the plant.

When you go back tell Colin we've started half
hours. Cecil's first.

DEZZIE: Right.

BLAKEY exits to the bread plant. DEZZIE finds some change and goes to the phone. He dials.

(*On phone.*) Nance... it's me... Hello luv. I were thinking, you know, what if I nip home about half ten eh? ... Yeah, no, I ain't got time for a bath... I've got to get back, an' all – don't forget... Yeah, oooh, you're my little badger... Tarra... love you... tarra.

Enter NELLIE. He looks significantly worse than when we last saw him. He is carrying his cream nylon shirt, but is naked from the waist up. The hairs on his body are matted with dough.

Put a shirt on Walter! This is a restaurant!

NELLIE: Lost me vest.

DEZZIE: You what?

NELLIE: I can't find me vest!

DEZZIE: Ha, ha. You're for the high jump if that's gone in the mix Walter.

NELLIE: It'll come out at tinning up.

DEZZIE: You hope.

NELLIE slips his shirt on but doesn't button it up. He finds his mug and a tea bag and brews up. He sits and takes out his pack of sandwiches and unwraps them. He looks at them unenthusiastically.

What you got there Walter?

NELLIE: Cheese.

DEZZIE: Nice. (*Beat.*) Do you want a ham sandwich?

NELLIE smiles broadly and rubs his head.

Here. Tek an apple an' all. If you want.

(*Conspiratorially.*) I'm nipping home on my half hour.

NELLIE takes a ham sandwich and an apple.

NELLIE: Ta.

DEZZIE takes a cigarette and lights up. NELLIE watches hoping to be offered a cigarette, but DEZZIE has drawn the line. NELLIE takes one of his own and DEZZIE lights it for him.

DEZZIE: What are we gonna do with you Walter? (*Beat.*) You're bombed out, aren't yer?

NELLIE says nothing, but rubs his face. Enter LANCE looking terrible, but energised by physical work. He is carrying, at arm's length, a vest caked in dough.

LANCE: Excuse me Dezzie, er... Nellie isn't it? Yes, the chargehand told me to give this to you.

NELLIE: My vest.

NELLIE puts the vest on, making no attempt to clean off the dough.

LANCE: (*To DEZZIE.*) The chargehand also asked me to tell you, Dezzie, that your smoke is over, er... apparently.

LANCE runs his burnt fingers under the cold tap.

DEZZIE: Me?

LANCE: I think so. What he actually said was "Tell that fucking deckie to get his arse back on the plant."

DEZZIE: Huh, I'm the only deckie around here. I'll mek you a cup of tea first Lance.

LANCE: Oh excellent. Thank you very much.

DEZZIE: I bet you didn't bring tea bags. How do you take your tea?

LANCE: Orally.

DEZZIE: Ha, you've livened up!

LANCE: Yes, I've taken a few chemicals intravenously, and I've had approved medical instruments up the arse, but with tea, it's definitely the mouth.

DEZZIE: Ha! Listen to him!

LANCE: I tell you that oven is not exactly a Baby Belling is it?

DEZZIE: (*To LANCE.*) Aye, it's a big un alright. Well, have a good smoke. I'll leave you two together. I'm sure you've got things to talk about.

DEZZIE exits. LANCE sits opposite NELLIE, and makes eye contact. NELLIE looks away, rubbing his head.

LANCE: Do you prefer Walter or Nellie?

NELLIE: Walter.

LANCE: Are you taking a 'smoke' Walter, or is this your half hour break?

NELLIE: Half hour.

LANCE: Excellent. So that means we won't be disturbed. I'm beginning to see how things work around here. I've got to go back onto the plant before anyone else can take a smoke. That's correct, yeah?

NELLIE: Yeah.

LANCE: So, we're going to be alone then?

NELLIE: Yeah.

LANCE: Excellent. Would it be possible to touch you for a cigarette?

NELLIE panics. He rubs his face not knowing what to say.

I normally eschew the weed, on health grounds naturally, but in situations like this the pressure of social conformity is greater than my will to live.

NELLIE, with great difficulty, releases a cigarette, and lights it for him.

I'm using 'will to live' there as a figure of speech naturally – having raged unsuccessfully against the dying of the light several years ago.

NELLIE: What are they learning you at school?

LANCE: I'm not a student Walter. I'm not at school. I'm here to see you. I can't tell you Walter, being dead has made a significant difference to my life. I have no concerns about my health, and I groom less. (*Beat.*) It is very opportune for me – being 'on a smoke' whilst you are taking your half hour. Alone in the canteen. It is quite perfect. One might even say designed. I feared that I would have to corner you in the lavatory or steal thirty seconds in the mixing room, just to be with you.

Pause.

Are you prepared Walter?

NELLIE: Eh?

LANCE: That is exactly what I said! How can one prepare? Death is the only real adventure. Planning, preparation, making ready – all tosh!

A willing acquiescence with fate is all that one
can reasonably contribute. (*Beat.*) I have told
them but they take very little notice of me.
I said take him, snatch him away, suddenly.
Why go to the expense of sending a messenger?
Do you realise, Walter, to send me here
has required eight signatures on two separate
requisitions. One for the exceptional
expenditure incurred, and one for a four-
day visa.

NELLIE: Where are you from?

LANCE: The other side. From across the metaphorical
water.

NELLIE: What? Grimsby?

LANCE: No Walter. The land of living souls and
rotting bodies. The next world.

NELLIE: Ger away. You're mad.

LANCE: Ah! It is true that I am chosen for this role
because I am, so I understand, perceived to be
mildly eccentric, but that is functional. The living
dismiss me as a madman, leaving only my clients
to take me seriously. And you, Walter, are a client.

NELLIE: You're not a student then?

LANCE: I'm a messenger. Your time is up, Walter.
They've made a decision at last. An all-night
meeting. A compromise solution was suggested
which, though not ideal, did not damage the
long-term objectives of either party. There's a
place for you now. Provision has been made.
Your er... loyalty to this company, and all-round
contribution to society, albeit in the narrow area

of bread mass production, served you well.
The committee actually calculated how many
loaves you've mixed in the forty-five years
you've worked here. Two hundred and twenty
million. That's an awful lot of toast Walter!

NELLIE: Who worked that out?

LANCE: Oh, one of the number crunchers. They're
very pleased with you. All that bread! Ha! It's a
mountain Walter! The decision, in the end, was
unanimous – a very rare thing. The committee
are already discussing the merits of another
case. Walter, trust me, it's not as terrible as it
sounds. I know where you're going. It's not
perfect, but it could be worse. Let's just say,
there are more ovens here – comprenez?

NELLIE: Na.

LANCE: You are going to die Walter. Tonight. It'll be
quick, and, thankfully, there'll be hardly any mess.

*LANCE stands, collects his things together and exits to the plant.
NELLIE watches him go. He rubs his head, deeply confused. Enter
COLIN, a bit worse for wear.*

COLIN: (*Sanctimonious.*) Bread's big Nellie. (*Beat.*)
I said the bread's coming out big Nellie. (*Beat.*)
Coming out fucking huge.

NELLIE: Yeah?

COLIN: Yeah. Is it going in big?

NELLIE: Blakey's got the prover too hot. (*To COLIN.*)
Is it going in big?

COLIN: Ger a grip Nellie! I just asked you that!
If a lid comes off and jams the oven we'll all be

for the high jump. Your lass won't stand for you not working. She'll move you back into the garden shed like before. That's where Blakey will get you.

NELLIE: You want Blakey's job don't yer?

COLIN: Eh? Got nowt to do with you Nellie. Who's put that in your head? There's no jobs going and you know it.

NELLIE: There's mine.

COLIN: Yours? I wouldn't do eighty hours a week. Anyhow, you've got another five year here, ain't yer?

NELLIE: Yeah.

COLIN: Well then, what you on about?

COLIN reads the paper, obscuring NELLIE from his POV.

Plays hell with your skin does mixing. Look at you. Dermatitis. You on half hours?

NELLIE: Yeah. (*Beat.*) That student's a right one.

COLIN: Aye, fruit and nut if you ask me.

NELLIE: Do you think he's been let out of De la Pole?

COLIN lowers his paper sharply.

COLIN: I couldn't give a fuck if he was from Mars, Nellie. He's like all the others. He'll do one shift, two shifts, maybe a week, and then we'll never see the cunt again. Waste of space, if you ask me. What's your star sign Nellie?

NELLIE: Eh?

COLIN: What are you? Gemini, Taurus, Aquarius?

NELLIE looks blank.

When's your birthday?

NELLIE: Eleventh of May.

COLIN: Taurus. (*Reading.*) Now is the time for fresh plans and new horizons. Take the bull of opportunity by the horns. Travel opportunities will present themselves with the prospect of exotic locations and equally extraordinary peoples. Finance – seeds planted now...

The drone of the plant stops suddenly with a sharp crack and a duller thud. NELLIE stands involuntarily. COLIN continues reading, not seeing NELLIE's reaction. The oven lurches, and bangs, lurches and bangs, and stops again.

... will bear fruit at a later date. Leave affairs of the heart until the favourable ascent of Venus pours light on your every romantic endeavour.

A muted, tired, alarm bell sounds on the plant.

What's up?

NELLIE opens the door. The alarm bell sounds louder.

NELLIE: Oven's jammed.

To black.

Scene 2

Later in the shift. The clock now shows just after ten. CECIL is sitting in the canteen alone. PETER enters. They acknowledge each other without speaking. PETER approaches the table and inspects a chair, cleaning it of dough. Unseen by PETER, CECIL makes a feint to grab PETER's balls, but does not go through with the grab. PETER becomes suspicious and conspicuously does not turn his back on CECIL. A strange dance ensues. PETER checks out another chair, all the time suspicious of CECIL. He checks the chair which had previously been sat on by NELLIE, tries to brush it down, picks a bit of dough off it, and then kicks it out of the way. He sits on the same side of the table as CECIL, picks up the cards and starts dealing four hands of thirteen card brag. CECIL picks up his cup, stands and ostentatiously backs towards the boiler.

CECIL: (*Teasing/ knowing.*) Not eating Peter?

PETER: My Chicken Kiev's stuck in the fucking oven, ain't it.

CECIL: Ha, oh yes. Lovely. Maybe a good thing. You can't overcook Chicken Kiev. (*Beat.*) Would you like a sarnie?

PETER: Fish paste? Yeah, great. Ta, Cecil. I blame Dezzie.

CECIL: Heart's in the right place.

PETER: Huh, if he had a brain he'd be dangerous.

PETER bites into the sandwich.

Oh God, there's nowt worse than a fish paste sarnie, is there?

CECIL: Oh no, that's not strictly true. Lot of things worse than a fish paste sandwich. You could fly into a mountain in a light aircraft.

65

PETER: I worry about you Cecil. What d'yer reckon to this bloke Lance?

CECIL: Oh we've 'ad 'em 'ere before. "NAAFI" we used to call 'em in the navy. "No aptitude and fuck-all interest". Oh yes.

PETER: What d'yer reckon – De la Pole?

CECIL: Oh yes, affirmative. Medical institution of some description – definitely.

PETER nods and sorts his cards.

We 'ad an 'eadcase here before. We called him Batley Dracula.

PETER: What d'yer call him that for?

CECIL: Cos he come from Batley. He did one shift, didn't like it. Next day he tried to hold up the Barclays Bank on Cott Road with a turnip wrapped in a carrier bag.

PETER: Now you've got to be mad to do that.

CECIL: Oh yes. (*Beat.*) A sane man would have used a carrot... or a cucumber. Oh, yes. It's a fine line. Madness, sanity, sadness, manity.

Enter LANCE and DEZZIE.

PETER: Eh up, here they are! Clumsy arsed bastards!

CECIL: (*Standing suddenly.*) Here, sit down Dezzie before you knock the table over.

PETER grabs CECIL's balls hard from behind and squeezes.

Aaaaagh! Oh, lovely shot! Oh, come at me out of the sun! Two – one after seven hours and everything to play for! Ohhhh, yes, lovely.

LANCE washes his hands and then stands looking up at the bread plant from inside the canteen. DEZZIE sits straight down and lights a cigarette.

DEZZIE: It weren't me Cecil. I'm gentle with them lids, and I trained up Lance here proper.

PETER: Who the fuck fucked up then?

DEZZIE: Dunno. I don't get paid to think. Your chicken meal will be doing nicely.

PETER: Fuck off.

DEZZIE: Fish paste eh? If you'd ever worked on trawlers – you wouldn't eat fish paste.

PETER: (*Resigned.*) Go on then put me off me food.

DEZZIE: Well, fish paste is mainly skate, you see.

PETER: So?

DEZZIE: Well, when your average deckie's been away at sea for a couple of weeks he gets a bit frisky like. And yer skate, as it happens, is not a bad fuck.

CECIL: Ha, marvellous! Is that right Dezzie, you can fuck a fish!?

DEZZIE: First trip I made, I were about seventeen, the mate called me over. He said, "Son, bring me one of them there skate, will yer. I fancy a shag." I said, "Does it matter which?" He said, "Yeah – bring me a good looking one."

CECIL: Ha, lovely!

PETER: 'Kin deckies!

DEZZIE: Eh, er... Peter, Cecil tells me you're selling your car like.

PETER: D'yer wannit?

DEZZIE: Na, can't drive mesen. But I've got a pal who'll dump it in dock for you for twenny quid.

PETER: Why would I want me car dumped in fishdock?

DEZZIE: Who said owt about *fish*dock?

PETER: Oh 'kinell. WHY!?

CECIL: Insurance, oh yes.

PETER: What meks you think it's insured?

CECIL: Ah! Ho ho! Crucial point that Dezzie.

DEZZIE: Sorry. Just trying to help.

CECIL: Are you gonna go home then Dezzie? I'll cover for you. You can take your time now – lovely!

DEZZIE: I don't know what Blakey's gonna want us to do, do I.

CECIL: (*Standing up.*) I'll go then. Lend us your crash helmet. I'm not getting much.

DEZZIE: Shut it will yer! You're talking about my missus.

PETER: (*Dealing a fresh hand.*) You in Dezzie?

DEZZIE: Aye.

PETER: Sir Lancelot? Eh, put your sword down and come over here, and let us tek some money off yer. You look like you've gorra bit.

LANCE: I don't mind joining in. Thank you.

During the next CECIL picks his cards up one by one. The others wait until the deal is done and then sort all thirteen at once.

PETER: Thirteen card brag.

LANCE: That's just like three card brag except I've got to make up four hands – right?

DEZZIE: That's right.

LANCE: So do I have to put my best hand first?

PETER: What? Yeah – your first hand has to be your best hand.

DEZZIE: But it doesn't have to be your best possible hand.

CECIL: The skill in this game is mekking four half-way decent hands.

DEZZIE: So if you've got a crap hand all round, the best thing you can do is mek three *really* crap hands but keep a good hand till last. That way you might win one at least.

PETER: Don't listen to him. He schooled yer how to put yer fucking lids on.

DEZZIE: Nowt wrong with our lids! I've told yer. The bread was big going in, weren't it Lance?

LANCE: Yes, yes, it was actually. Well, it's not for me to say, but I do remember Dez remarking on the turgescent nature of the doughs.

DEZZIE: Did I?

LANCE: Yes, you did Dez. "Bugger me they're big," is what you actually said.

PETER: That right Dezzie?

DEZZIE: Yeah. Big 'olemeal was huge.

CECIL: (*Having picked up his cards.*) Tragic, tragic. What a steaming pile of shite.

LANCE: (*Laying his cards.*) Four fours.

PETER: (*Throwing in a weaker hand.*) 'Kinnel.

CECIL: (*Throwing in a weaker hand.*) Four fours! Oh lovely!

DEZZIE: Pral o' threes.

They all laugh. PETER and CECIL throw in poor hands.

LANCE: Jack, queen, king.

PETER: I don't fucking believe it!

CECIL: (*Throwing in a useless hand.*) Are you gonna give her a ring? Yes, go on Dezzie.

The others throw in useless hands.

DEZZIE: Should I?

LANCE: Pair of kings.

PETER: He split three kings! (*Throwing in a useless hand.*) Ha, yours.

CECIL: Oh yes. She'll be running a bath now. What's the time?

DEZZIE: Just gone ten. Yeah, she will.

LANCE: Queen high.

PETER: (*Throwing in a useless hand.*) You get two pence off everyone now. Tax free.

They all cough up their debts to LANCE. DEZZIE goes to the phone. He dials. It rings and rings – no answer. LANCE gathers his money.

70

CECIL: Keep it ringing Dezzie. She'll just've got out of the bath.

PETER: (*Stands.*) Where's yer phone?

DEZZIE: Er... dunno.

PETER: (*Marking out the steps.*) It'll be at bottom of stairs. Well, hang on then, hang on, she'll be half way down, wait... wait... wait, now!

DEZZIE: Hello luv!

They all cheer.

(*As much to the lads as to NANCY.*) Were you in the bath? ... You're standing at bottom of stairs mekking a puddle.

CECIL: Oooh, if I could be that puddle.

DEZZIE: Eh, ... the oven's buggered. We're doing nowt down here. We don't know what's happened... I might be here till seven in morning... Dunno – a tin's got stuck I think... We don't know yet. So, I thought I might come home, you know for a couple of hours.

CECIL: (*Quietly.*) Kaaaw.

DEZZIE: (*On the phone.*) Cecil said he'd cover for us... Yeah, what do you think? ... Yeah, I'll get a bottle of wine from the beer-off shall I? ... Na! Mr Beckett won't know about it. I've got to come back after though.

CECIL: After! D'yer hear that? After! Ho, ho.

DEZZIE turns his back and continues talking on the phone.

PETER: What do you do Lance?

LANCE: Well, I'm a student of social and economic history, and I dabble a little in antiques, ephemera, collectables.

PETER: Collectables?

LANCE: Yes, I buy quirky items. Pieces with some historical interest.

PETER: What would you give us for Cecil then?

LANCE: Ha! Very good, er... no, this is a good example of my stock.

LANCE takes an old, bent and rusty nail from his pocket. He holds it up in front of PETER.

This is a nail from the *H.M.S. Bounty.*

PETER: Ah! So that's the nail what Trevor Howard hung his hat on!

CECIL: Oh no, Charles Laughton.

LANCE: I got this from a colleague...

PETER: Eh up he's got colleagues!

CECIL: Ho, ho!

LANCE: ... who imports historical ephemera, and I sell on.

PETER: What's that worth then?

LANCE: This one? Well, five pounds.

PETER: Five quid! It's a nail from a fucking bombsite!

LANCE: Pitcairn's Island actually.

CECIL: Ha! I'll give you fifty p. I've always liked Charles Laughton.

LANCE: (*To CECIL.*) Four pounds.

CECIL: Sixty p.

LANCE: Done.

CECIL: Eh!? What?

PETER: Ha, ha, pay the man. You offered.

CECIL hands over the money willingly, enjoying the joke.

CECIL: Clark Gable he was good too. Bit left-handed though I reckon. Oh yes.

DEZZIE: (*On the phone.*) Tarra then love.

DEZZIE puts the phone down and sits at the table.

(*To PETER.*) Lekky.

PETER: You what?

DEZZIE: We're on lekky – for the hot water.

PETER: What – an immersion tank?

DEZZIE: I don't know. What's that look like?

CECIL: It's a big copper tank – usually in a cupboard.

DEZZIE: A big tank in a cupboard?

PETER: Usually at top of stairs.

DEZZIE: I can't remember.

CECIL: Ring her up and find out.

DEZZIE: Aye, I think I will.

DEZZIE looks for change in his pockets.

CECIL: (*Offering him a five pence piece.*) Here.

DEZZIE: Ta Cecil – you're a diamond.

PETER: What are you gonna do about it then Cecil?

CECIL: 'Bout what?

PETER: Not getting any.

CECIL: Don't know – what can I do?

PETER: Well you could have a good night out with me one night. (*Beat.*) Come down the White Hart.

CECIL: I'm not paying for it. I've never had to pay for it. Oh no.

DEZZIE: (*On the phone.*) Nance, it's me again. You know the water heating, yeah, is it like in a tank in a cupboard... It is! Ah.

(*Addressing the shift.*) It's an immersion tank!

(*On the phone.*) Put it on Nance, I'll have a bath when I get in. Tarra Mrs Badger... love you... bye.

CECIL: So you've got a tank then Dezzie?

DEZZIE: Looks that way don't it.

CECIL: You wanna fit some wooden slats over the top. I did that for our lass about ten year back. She liked that a great deal. Airs the washing in there she does. Oh yes, she liked it. Liked that a great deal. Oh yes.

DEZZIE: You alright, Lance son?

LANCE: Excellent thank you Dezzie.

DEZZIE: They're not having a go at you then?

LANCE: Oh no, I've just sold Cecil one of my *Bounty* nails. I do have a couple more.

DEZZIE: I wouldn't mind one of them. Piece of history that. How much do you want for it?

LANCE: Well, for complex social reasons which I won't go into, the price has been established at sixty p.

DEZZIE: Is it real?

LANCE: Certainly. A professor friend of mine at Hull University confirmed their authenticity last Wednesday lunchtime.

DEZZIE: (*Paying him.*) There you go then.

LANCE: Thank you Dezzie. I've been meaning to ask. Is it possible that the oven jamming might be the fault of the mixer? Nellie's fault?

CECIL: Na, Nellie's a star, oh yes.

PETER: It's Blakey's fault. He's got the prover too hot, and the oven too fast.

Enter BLAKEY, NELLIE, COLIN in that order. BLAKEY's looking severe, and NELLIE sheepish. COLIN is fighting back a smile. BLAKEY gets his mug and makes some tea. COLIN and NELLIE sit at the second table.

CECIL: I was just saying Nellie. You're a star aren't you? Oh yes.

BLAKEY: (*Inadvertently looking at DEZZIE.*) We've got a jammed tin.

DEZZIE: Well all my tins were put on right.

BLAKEY: It wasn't you Dezzie. I reckon one of the mixes was wrong.

NELLIE rubs his face and stares at the table.

PETER: (*Turning to NELLIE.*) What did you do Nellie?

NELLIE, desperately ashamed, stares at the table, rubs his face and looks gormlessly at the floor.

Well!

COLIN: Double yeast probably!

PETER: How the fuck did you manage that?

CECIL: Eh, er... calm down Peter. Anyone can make a mistake.

PETER: Every fucking shift there's a Nellie cock-up! His vest got in a tin tonight. His vest! Yeah!? (*To CECIL.*) Imagine your lass going to Hammonds and buying a twenny-eight ounce loaf cos she fancies a bit of toast, and when she gets home and she finds she's got Nellie's vest in a bag. Eh!?

CECIL: Our lass don't like toast.

PETER: (*Deflates.*) Oh fuck off Cecil.

CECIL: And she's banned from Hammonds. Oh yes.

DEZZIE: How come she got banned from Hammonds?

CECIL: I don't want to tell you Dezzie. It was a terrible business. Dreadful.

Silence.

DEZZIE: So you've got a jammed lid Blakey?

BLAKEY: Yeah.

CECIL: Have you shut the burners off?

COLIN: Yeah, course.

DEZZIE: What happens now then? Can we go home?

COLIN: With the burners off the oven'll tek eight, nine hours to cool down before the fitters can work on it.

BLAKEY: And another five hours to get back to temperature before it'll bek bread.

CECIL: We might as well go then. Oh, yes. Call it a day. There's nowt to do. I don't want to clean. Oh no.

DEZZIE picks up his helmet. COLIN hunts in his bag for his union rule book.

BLAKEY: Peter?

PETER: Well of course I wanna go home don't I? But I'm not gonna go home if going home means I don't get paid – am I?! If we stay here they gorra pay us ain't they? So I'll stay if 'ave to – but I'd rather go home.

BLAKEY: Dezzie?

CECIL: Dezzie wants to go home. Don't you Dezzie? Given the choice between cleaning and going home. Tonight, he would choose to go home. Wouldn't you Dezzie?

DEZZIE: (*Mock equivocal.*) I'm easy.

CECIL and PETER laugh.

COLIN: (*Rule book in hand.*) We can't be made to clean. The agreement is that the management employs each of us – (*Reading.*) – "as bread plant operatives and is obligated to provide work of that nature within the defined and agreed hours".

BLAKEY: Other work's possible.

COLIN: Only following negotiation. And there's no management here to negotiate is there? Eh? You're not management.

BLAKEY: I could ring Beckett.

PETER: (*Challenging.*) You not told Beckett yet?!

BLAKEY: No.

PETER: What – no-one knows this has happened? What about Skeltons? They're sending an artic tonight.

BLAKEY: The artic's not due till one in morning.

PETER: Why ain't yer told Beckett?

BLAKEY: What do I tell him?

PETER: Well, tell him to send a fitter out.

BLAKEY: Oh aye, easy. Hello Mr Beckett, oven's jammed! I might as well ring Calvert at Bradford while I'm at it.

PETER: (*Standing.*) Oh I see. You'll get the blame for this won't yer. Not Nellie. If Beckett gets wind of this you can wave goodbye to that job at Bradford can't yer? Yeah, well tough. We wanna go home. So ring him up. Here's five p.

PETER throws a five pence piece onto the table.

BLAKEY: You ring him up and tell him the plant's fucked. Go on!

BLAKEY pushes the coin back towards PETER.

PETER: Alright I will.

PETER, slightly embarrassed, heads towards the phone with no real intention of making the call.

BLAKEY: Tell him there's a jammed tin. Tell him the burners are turned off. Tell him it'll take eight hours to cool down. Tell him he'll be lucky if he gets it going again.

PETER: Steady on will yer! I've only got five p.

BLAKEY: Tell him every bombed out bit of metal in that fucking reel oven will shrink, crack and split. Tell him he'd better get our P45s sorted out an' all. Oh, and while you're on, ask him for that hundred and fifty quid sub you need. Now's gorra be a good time.

PETER: You're not serious are yer? You're having me on. This place is a fucking gold mine. All they got to do is point us stupid fuckers in the right direction, and then the next day go down to the bank with the money. They wouldn't close us down?

DEZZIE: (*Standing and approaching.*) Ah, but Peter, you're forgetting all the new investment at Bradford. You see, if you've just bought a new car, you're not going to hang onto your old banger just because it still goes, are you? Eh? Think about it.

PETER: The great wise deckie speaks.

CECIL: He's right. Oh yes.

COLIN: Yeah, that's the end of this place.

CECIL: (*To BLAKEY.*) Well?

BLAKEY: Fine. You wanna go. Go home. I'll tell Beckett.

DEZZIE has his helmet on now.

DEZZIE: We're getting paid yeah?

BLAKEY: Course.

DEZZIE: I'm off!

PETER: Sit yourself down Dezzie!

DEZZIE remains standing, helmet on – undecided.

What'll the fitters do tomorrow, when it's cooled off?

BLAKEY: Go in and knock the tin free.

PETER: Go *in*? What? Go in the oven?

BLAKEY: Yeah.

NELLIE: There's a door.

DEZZIE: I've never seen a door.

PETER: Well you don't know where your own fucking house is do you?

BLAKEY: There's a door about twenty yards down on the window side.

PETER: What's it for?

BLAKEY: Servicing, maintenance. It hasn't been opened for five years.

NELLIE: I'll go in.

PETER: You what Nellie?

NELLIE: I'll go in. I've been in before.

PETER: When?

NELLIE: 'Bout ten year after it were put in. Tin got stuck. Mr Beckett told me to go in and look for it.

PETER: You'll be going up chimneys next Nellie.

NELLIE: Found it.

DEZZIE: Can you breathe in there?

NELLIE: Held me breath.

PETER: Fucking pearl diving now!

CECIL: How did you know where it was?

NELLIE: You can't see, you have to feel.

PETER: Pin the tail on the donkey!

CECIL: Is it nice in there Nellie? Eh? You know – nice.

NELLIE: Black.

COLIN: Hang on, hang on! Look, I don't like the sound of this. None of us are going nowhere near that oven. That's a fitter's job. They'll send a team down from Bradford tomorrow and that'll be that. We go home now, on full pay, and be finished with it. This ain't our problem, it's management's. 'Bout time they started mekkin some decisions any road.

PETER: What do you know about plans for this place Colin, eh?

COLIN: You what?

PETER: Yeah, you're close to management.

COLIN: What's that supposed to mean?

PETER: Oh come on, we all know you're half way up Beckett's arse.

COLIN stands suddenly violently pushing his chair back. He eyeballs PETER who flinches back frightened.

COLIN: Shut it Peter, alright!

PETER: Suits you nicely this don't it? Blakey has a fuck-up. Bradford'll close the plant, Blakey won't get the chargehand job at Bradford. In like Flynn, and twice as fucking dodgy, tupperware man, the man of the moment!

COLIN: Don't push it Peter.

PETER: I'll push all your fucking buttons until summat lights up.

COLIN: Alright. This place is finished. There's no point. I mean give me one reason why I should, why anybody should, give a flying fuck. It's history, ancient history. (*To BLAKEY.*) If you don't want to tell Beckett, that's your business.

BLAKEY: I didn't know you'd applied for chargehand at Bradford?

COLIN: What if I have? There's no law against it. No law against bettering yourself. It ain't just me I've gorra look after you know.

BLAKEY: Well, well. Fuck me sideways.

COLIN: I'll clock out. I'll give mesen a flier.

COLIN leaves. He leaves the door to the bread plant open.

NELLIE: I'll go in the oven.

PETER: Shut up Nellie! It's not your fault.

CECIL: That's not what you said a minute ago.

PETER: I blame you Blakey.

CECIL: Oh dear.

PETER: You were running the plant too fast.
Running Nellie too fast. Cos you hate it here.
You wanted to go home. You always want to
go home. As soon as you get here you wanna
go home.

Unnoticed, NELLIE leaves the canteen.

Don't get me wrong I don't love it here. D'yer
think I like coming in here on a Sunday? I've
gorra come here. I need to come here. I ain't got
no choice. And do you think I'm not fucking sick
of it after sixty hours? Now if you don't wanna
chargehand you should pass it on to someone
who does – like Colin. But you can't do that can
you? Cos your big bollocks Blakey aren't you?
And you like that, don't you? You're nobody
Blakey. You're like me – you're nowt, hourly
paid, wage labour. You won't get Bradford cos
you're a lairy bastard and they know it, and they
like Colin. And you won't get work nowhere else
with your record. I wouldn't care, but I need this
fucking shithole! You've fucked this place tonight
Blakey! You've fucked it for me.

CECIL: You're at top pitch son, settle down.

PETER: (*To BLAKEY.*) You just don't fucking realise,
do you?! You don't know what you've done!!

DEZZIE: Now come on Peter. Leave it alone.

PETER: I can't believe this is all over one fucking, poxy, jammed tin!!

BLAKEY: I'm gonna go in and free the tin.

DEZZIE: You what?

BLAKEY: I can find the tin and free it. We'll clear the run and start again.

DEZZIE: Hang on. You're not serious are you?

CECIL: What's the temperature of the oven Blakey?

BLAKEY: I don't know.

PETER: You what? You're the fucking chargehand and you don't know the temperature?

BLAKEY: Maximum. Full burn. It's all about speed. If you want a light bake, send it round quick, twenty-five minutes a cycle, like tonight. Look, what I'm saying is Beckett's not in till eight in the morning. That gives us nearly nine hours and we've only got eight hours' production to do. If we fix it in the next hour no-one will know anything about it.

CECIL: I'm getting excited. Very tense. Oh God!

DEZZIE: I'm lost.

CECIL: What Blakey is suggesting Dezzie, is that he goes into the oven now while it's still hot, finds the tin and wraps it round Nellie's head. Good idea.

PETER: Where is Nellie?

DEZZIE: He went out a bit back.

BLAKEY: What? I didn't see him go nowhere.

PETER: Oh fuck!

CECIL: Oh shit!

PETER: Oh fucking hell, no. Walter, no!

DEZZIE: What? What's up?

PETER: Oh fuck no! Oh no, he wouldn't would he?

CECIL: He would, he would! Oh yes, he would.

PETER: Walter!

PETER flies out of the canteen up the steps and onto the plant. BLAKEY throws a towel into the sink and puts the cold tap on.

BLAKEY: Come on!

All except LANCE rush up to the plant. The door is left open. LANCE walks over and closes the door. He finds a paper and begins to do the crossword. Muffled cries of "Nellie! Nellie!" and "Walter! Walter!" drift down from the bread plant. Enter COLIN, rather sheepishly. COLIN stops on seeing LANCE, and then continues toward the steel table to collect the tupperware box which he had left behind. The door is left open.

COLIN: (*Embarrassed.*) Left my boxes. Where are the others?

LANCE: They're all up on the plant. Something to do with Nellie. I don't think we'll be disturbed.

COLIN: You what?

LANCE: Nothing, nothing. I'm just er... stuck on a crossword clue. (*Reading.*) Postman loses bag?

COLIN: How many letters?

LANCE: A bagful. Ha! I didn't think I'd trick you with that one. Not you.

COLIN: What's your game?

LANCE: I'm glad you asked Colin. You see, I've been sent here, to see you. I stand before you as a messenger...

COLIN: You're sat down.

LANCE stands and walks to the door and closes it deliberately.

LANCE: Ah yes, observational skills. Excellent. Colin, the thing is, I've been watching you. Assessment is part of my role. You are under-utilised. You can mix, you could chargehand I guess, but rather stupidly you took on the role of shop steward, a function for which you are, in all respects, profoundly unsuitable. For a start, shop stewards should always be Welsh. Secondly they should have at least some sympathy with the international socialist movement. Only death will bring you promotion...

COLIN: Shut the fuck up, will you!

LANCE: Jesus was a carpenter...

COLIN: Shut it!

LANCE: ...but his father was a baker, metaphorically speaking.

COLIN grabs him by the lapels and about the throat. There is banging and muffled cries from inside the oven offstage. He backs him up against the wall stage right.

COLIN: I said knock it on the head, you crazy cunt!

LANCE: (*Muffled, struggling.*) I'm only trying to help. I've been sent to warn you, that's all!

COLIN: You're no student. (*Shouting.*) You're from fucking De la Pole aren't yer?! You're an 'eadcase proper! Aren't yer? Aren't yer!!??

LANCE, unable to talk, nods agreement to save his skin. COLIN ejects him to the plant and slams the door on him. He finally packs his tupperware boxes into each other. LANCE looks in at the window too scared to come back in. COLIN goes to the phone. He takes out a piece of paper from his wallet and dials. During the next there is more banging and muffled cries off.

Hello... Mrs Beckett? ... Oh sorry to bother you at this late hour, on a Sunday, but could I have a quick word with Mr Beckett please? ... It's Colin Dawson from the bread plant... He's here now? What – on the bread plant? ... Er, I've not seen him... He's been here all night, since eight? ... Definitely not Mrs Beckett, we couldn't miss him could we... Er, well, no, er goodnight, and sorry to bother you... No. Like I say – I'm certain of it – he's not been here Mrs Beckett... Tarra.

He puts the phone down. Enter NELLIE, having climbed the stairs up to the canteen. He is doing up his flies.

NELLIE: Colin.

COLIN: (*Indicates his tupperware box.*) I forgot them. Our lass would've gone spare. Eh, Nellie, have you seen Beckett tonight?

NELLIE: Here?

COLIN: Yeah, on the plant?

NELLIE: No. He wouldn't come here on a Sunday evening. (*Beat.*) He'll be shagging that lass from custards.

COLIN: Eh? That's just a rumour though innit?

I mean, Beckett's sixty-five ain't he? That lass ain't twenny-two.

NELLIE: Na. He's always gor a young un sorted out.

COLIN: (*Muted, but intense.*) Shit!

NELLIE: He's 'ad 'em all, 'as Mr Beckett. Them on custards, pasties, apple turnovers, ... pork pies, oh aye, he's not choosy. (*Beat.*) And the eccles cakes. He had the pick of the lasses on the eccles cakes. When I fost come here, I were about fourteen, he said to me, "You'll do well here, Walter as long as you keep your prick out the payroll." He said that to everyone, just so's he could have the pick for hissen. Aye.

COLIN: What about Mrs Beckett? Does she know?

NELLIE: No! He don't tell her nothing! It's not a proper marriage like that. (*Beat.*) Will they pull the plug Colin?

COLIN: What?

NELLIE: Bradford.

COLIN: Yeah, course.

NELLIE: Beckett'll look after you though won't he.

COLIN: Yeah! By rights.

NELLIE: But worrabout Blakey?

COLIN: Blakey's fucked. So's everyone here. Are you sure you ain't seen Beckett? He didn't come in to do them Skeltons' sheets did he?

NELLIE: Na. Like I said he'll be shagging...

COLIN: Alright! I fucking heard you fost time!

COLIN leaves, passing a glance at the phone. NELLIE is left on his own. He takes out his cigarettes, looks longingly at them, remembers he can only have two a shift and puts them back in his pocket. Then realising that the plant is finished, he takes them out again and lights up. He takes a drag and thoroughly enjoys it. Then he starts to worry. He stands on hearing the lads banging on the side of the oven.

BLAKEY/PETER: (*Off.*) Nellie!

Enter DEZZIE running.

DEZZIE: I gorra get me torch. What? What are you doing in here? Peter's in the oven looking for you! He's in the oven!!

NELLIE: I just went t'bog.

DEZZIE: Oh no!

DEZZIE exits running shouting.

(*Off.*) Stop! Stop! Nellie's in the canteen! Peter! Stop! Ger 'im out!

NELLIE sits with his head in his hands. CECIL is the first to enter, his clean whites now showing one or two black stripes.

CECIL: Huh! You're for it now Nellie. Oh yes.

NELLIE: I went t'bog.

CECIL: Oh no. I can't be doing with this excitement. Thought you was dead!

The others return. PETER runs in and turns the cold tap on. He is nursing fairly serious burns and is covered in black streaks from being inside the ovens. He goes straight to the sink and sticks his arms and head under the running cold tap. LANCE is nursing him.

BLAKEY: Where the fuck have you bin?

NELLIE: I just went t'bog.

BLAKEY: Well, why didn't you tell no-one? We thought you were in the fucking oven! You're daft enough!

NELLIE: I just went t'bog.

CECIL: Where did you go Nellie?

NELLIE: T'bog.

PETER: (*Spluttering under the tap.*) We bin in the fucking oven!

NELLIE: Well, I were in the bog.

BLAKEY: Peter 'ere's been in the oven looking for you, you daft bastard!

CECIL: Didn't find you though, Nellie. You must've been in the bog or somewhere.

DEZZIE: Yeah, Peter didn't find you.

CECIL: He found a couple of tourists in there wandering around lost. Unprepared they were, yes, very irresponsible.

NELLIE: Sorry Peter. I were in t'bog.

PETER: (*Still spluttering.*) Saw the tin though. Aye, it's down prover end.

BLAKEY: Prover end? That'd be big 'olemeal. Makes no sense that. You sure?

BLAKEY inspects his work sheets.

PETER: Yeah, it's on one of the bottom trays. All buckled up, and tray is skewed an' all. You'll need a crowbar. It's a two-man job.

CECIL: Lovely! Count me in!

DEZZIE: I'm not going in there.

CECIL: Yes you are Dezzie. You're the only one with a helmet.

BLAKEY: Walter, did you mix big 'olemeal?

NELLIE: No.

CECIL: Did you see your pie in there Peter?

PETER: It's not a pie, it's a Chicken Kiev.

CECIL: Your lass'll go spare.

PETER: She don't know I've gorrit. Nicked it from the fridge.

CECIL: Poor thing. It don't know whether it's coming or going, summer or winter.

PETER: You what?

CECIL: The pie.

PETER: It's not a fucking pie!

CECIL: Sorry. Just, it'll be confused. It's gone from extremes of cold to extremes of heat.

BLAKEY: (*To PETER.*) What do you think Peter?

PETER: Dunno. Might be easy. Knock it hard.

CECIL: Sweet. Lovely.

BLAKEY: Alright then. Walter, go to the basement and get me a crowbar from the fitter's room. And a lump hammer.

CECIL: Careful down there Nellie. They're fly buggers them mice.

NELLIE: Aye, I know.

BLAKEY: What's it like in there Peter?

NELLIE exits. PETER runs his head under the tap.

PETER: Fucking 'ot.

BLAKEY: You can see though?

PETER: Yeah, just. But you're best off keeping your eyes shut and feeling your way round. You gorra lie on your back – it's like working under a car.

BLAKEY: Right, you and Cecil go to despatch and ger as much sacking as you can find and twine an' all. Don't get nylon, it'll melt.

PETER: We'll fuckin melt before it does.

DEZZIE: I'll ring our lass. She'll be getting all wrinkly in that bath. (*To CECIL.*) Yeah, have you got...

CECIL: – No sorry Dez. You've cleaned me out.

BLAKEY: Dezzie, go and get the first-aid box from the back office. Cecil?

DEZZIE: You're not going in the oven are you Cecil?

CECIL: Oh yes. You don't need a record not to be able to get no work. Oh no. Just got to be slightly older than the next chap. Oh yes.

DEZZIE exits worried.

Nowt to lose is there. Can't afford to er... do nowt. Wouldn't know what to do with mysen at home. Our lass around all the time. I'll go in if you want Blakey. I can't go fishing every day,

can I? I mean if they shut this place that's it,
innit? I'll never work again. Not at my age. Our
lass wouldn't stand for it – me being at home
like. Oh no. Wouldn't work – me not working.
It's her place you see really. I'm never there am
I, 'cept when I'm in bed. I'm always here or
fishing, and I don't really like fishing, oh no.
I spend all the time walking when I'm fishing.
No-one ever nicks the rod. Not done. I like it
here. Well, you know how it is. If we get that
oven going this place might last another couple
of year, mightn't it? Blakey? What'd yer reckon?

BLAKEY: Oven'll go on for ever as long as it don't
cool down.

CECIL: What about Beckett though?

BLAKEY: Beckett don't get to know about nothing.

PETER: What? We just work through the sheets?

BLAKEY: Yeah, should finish about seven in morning.

PETER: Huh! We'll be back here at three. What
about the Skellies' artic? He'll be here in a few
hours and there'll be nowt for him.

BLAKEY: We'll do the Skellies' order fost and
leave our stuff till last.

PETER: You've got it all worked out, haven't you?

BLAKEY: Yeah. Yeah, I have. That's why I get paid
ten pence an hour more than you.

*PETER and CECIL exit. BLAKEY goes and makes himself a
tea, sits opposite LANCE and lights a cigarette.*

(*To LANCE.*) Are you enjoying yoursen?

LANCE: Enjoy? That's possibly the wrong word, but yes, I feel that generally speaking it is a positive experience. Yes.

BLAKEY: Where do you live Lance?

LANCE: Er... I have rooms in Willerby.

BLAKEY: Willerby eh? Very nice. Up near the hospital eh?

LANCE: I can see the hospital from my window. The others, will they be long?

BLAKEY: How do you mean?

LANCE: Will we be disturbed?

BLAKEY: Not for a couple of minutes, no.

LANCE: There's something I have to tell you.

BLAKEY: No.

LANCE: The reason I'm here...

BLAKEY: Shut it! Not wi' me pal! Alright? I've been told.

LANCE: Alright, I'm sorry.

BLAKEY: Look, now's as good a time as any, I've been meaning to ask yer, nowt to do with me really, but since I'm the chargehand mebbe it is. Anyhow, chances are I won't see you again. Them wrists of yours – why did you have a go at yourself?

Pause.

I was sort of relying on Dezzie to find out about you. You know, a couple of long night shifts on the ovens with nowt to do but talk. Twelve hours of cod war stories. I've known blokes get seasick listening to Dezzie. Look, what I'm trying to say is working on the oven there's nowt to do but talk. And you will talk. You'll be talking to Dezzie about things you haven't even dared think about for years, and then I'll come along tek you off for a smoke, and then Dezzie'll tell me all about yer. See what I'm saying? But with this cock-up, I'm gonna miss out on that little pleasure. So, you 'ad a go at yoursen. Why's that then?

LANCE: Yes, yes. Well, I don't know how to put this.

BLAKEY: Don't be shy about it. I might have been there mesen for all you know.

LANCE: My doctor, the consultant, calls it an absence of self.

BLAKEY: Oh aye?

LANCE: Fundamentally it is a desire to disappear, just not to be. I actually got to the point where it was difficult to look in the mirror.

BLAKEY: Scared there might be a toothbrush just waving around on its tod, eh?

LANCE: No, no. More...

BLAKEY: I know what you mean. Can't stand the fucking sight of yourself cos of what you've done. Used to get that a lot mesen. When I were inside.

LANCE: Yes, yes. So, I er, tried to finish it.

BLAKEY: What 'ad you done?

LANCE: Nothing. That is essentially the problem. I had done nothing. I haven't ever done anything really, until this. You know, I think I've got an aptitude for the ovens. I know it's defined as unskilled work, but I suspect it's not the sort of work that just anybody can do. And I can do it. That's very important to me. What about you? What did you do?

Enter CECIL, and PETER with sackcloth and twine.

BLAKEY: Six years. Well pal, when you go home this morning, you'll be too tired to look in the mirror.

CECIL: This'll do won't it Blakey?

BLAKEY: Good. Get yourself covered up then.

CECIL: How about soaking 'em fost?

LANCE: No, you'd just poach to death. Surely.

CECIL: Poached egg, lovely.

BLAKEY: (*To LANCE.*) You're not to say owt about this to no-one. Understand?

LANCE: Sure.

CECIL: Oh bloody hell I'm getting excited. I might die. Oh no, I can't be having that.

CECIL starts wrapping a tea towel around his head. PETER dresses CECIL in sackcloth. LANCE dresses BLAKEY in sackcloth, tearing it and forming a sackcloth suit which is tied to him with twine. BLAKEY rolls his sleeves down, buttons up his collar and wraps a spare t-shirt from his bag around his head. Enter DEZZIE and NELLIE.

DEZZIE: (*Clocking CECIL with the tea towel on his head.*) Bugger me, it's Lawrence of Arabia. Where's your camel lad?

BLAKEY: Have you got your torch Dezzie?

DEZZIE: Aye, in my bag.

DEZZIE gets the torch from his bag and hands it to BLAKEY.

(*To BLAKEY.*) What do you want us to do?

BLAKEY: You and Peter stand by the oven door. We'll give you a shout if we need you. Stay in here Walter.

NELLIE stands as if to protest. BLAKEY takes the lump hammer from him.

Stay in here!

LANCE: (*To BLAKEY.*) It might help to put a hat on.

PETER: (*To NELLIE.*) Lend him yer hat Nellie!

NELLIE doesn't look too keen.

He'll bon his 'ead otherwise. Won't he?

CECIL: Go on Nellie. Lend him yer hat.

NELLIE gives BLAKEY the hat. He puts it on.

BLAKEY: Thanks, pal.

Pause.

Right. Let's go.

They file out. CECIL, PETER, LANCE and DEZZIE. NELLIE stands in the doorway looking up at the plant. BLAKEY waits until the others have gone up the steps then he turns to NELLIE.

Call an ambulance. Tell them there's been an
accident. And stay in there!

*BLAKEY shoves him into the canteen and shuts the door on him.
NELLIE rings 999.*

NELLIE: (*On the phone.*) Ambulance... Rosedale
Street Bakehouse. Rosedale Street... Burns,
someone's got burnt bad... Ta.

*He puts the phone down. NELLIE turns and goes to sit down.
He rubs his head with his hands, surprised not to find his hat. He
lights a cigarette, but doesn't enjoy it. The banging starts on the
plant – it sounds muffled, distant. NELLIE stands and moves to
the doorway, listening. The banging continues. NELLIE paces.
Sits. Stands. Paces. Like a dog not allowed into the house he stands
on the threshold of the bread plant and then sits back down in the
canteen. The phone rings. NELLIE panics. He looks at the phone
ringing and then back to the plant.*

(*Like a child, nearly crying.*) It's Beckett. Mr Beckett.
It's Beckett. Oh no, it's Mr Beckett.

*NELLIE goes to the door, opens it and, standing on the threshold,
cries, not loudly but desperately, to the bread plant.*

Blakey! Blakey! It's Beckett. Oh no, please,
please no, not Beckett, please.

He turns back to the phone, picks it up and speaks.

Hello. Bread plant... Walter... aye... Oh hello
Mrs Grindley... Cecil? He's not here... No, he's in
the oven... yeah, he's gone in the oven... he
volunteered like... No, we got a jammed tin, so
he's gone in to free it up... Yeah, that's right he's
gone in to clear the tin... no, Blakey's gone in with

him... Yeah, he'll be alright, and if not I've already called an ambulance, just in case like... Aye alright... Oh aye, it'll still be hot, oh aye red hot but we've got him all dressed up in sackcloth like, so he shouldn't get burnt over much... Calm down Mrs Grindley... Oh aye, he'll be right as rain. I'll get him to ring yer when he comes out... tarra.

NELLIE sits again at the main table. Banging is heard off with occasional shouts of "You alright?" and "Keep talking to us". These shouts turn to "Come on that's enough" "Call it a day for fuck's sake". Three more bangs followed by a muffled cheer. NELLIE lifts his head and looks towards the door. Cheering off. NELLIE stands. Enter BLAKEY, CECIL, PETER, DEZZIE and LANCE. BLAKEY and CECIL have badly scorched overalls. They are jubilant. CECIL is carrying, in a gloved hand, a badly crumpled four piece tin with the remnants of burnt bread inside.

BLAKEY: That weren't too bad! Eh, Nellie!

CECIL: (*Handing over his ready meal, now a piece of charcoal.*) There's your pie Peter!

PETER: Do you want a bit?

BLAKEY: (*To LANCE who holds a bucket.*) Gi us some o' that water Lance.

BLAKEY sticks NELLIE's hat in the bucket and squeezes it out over CECIL's head.

CECIL: Gerr off! I'm in no need of that.

BLAKEY tosses the wet hat at the overjoyed NELLIE.

PETER: 'Ere Nellie! Cop 'od o' that!

CECIL: First wash it's had in ten year!

BLAKEY: Walter, take a skegg at this.

CECIL ceremoniously drops the offending tin and lid on the table. NELLIE comes over for a look.

It were right at this end.

PETER: This is a fucking big 'olemeal tin!

BLAKEY: D'yer hear that Nellie? The lid was on the big 'olemeal.

NELLIE digs out a burnt piece of bread and looks at it.

NELLIE: It's 'olemeal.

BLAKEY: Yeah. And you didn't do the big 'olemeal mix did yer?

NELLIE: No, I never.

BLAKEY: No, it were that Colin.

CECIL: You were on your first smoke weren't you Nellie?

PETER: Colin's put a double slammer of yeast in the fucking 'olemeal mix!

NELLIE: It weren't me then?

CECIL: No, it weren't you Nellie!

NELLIE: (*To BLAKEY.*) It weren't me!?

PETER kisses NELLIE like a footballer kissing a teammate.

BLAKEY: It weren't you!

NELLIE: It were Colin's mix?!

BLAKEY: Aye!

PETER: Whatsamatter Walter?

NELLIE: Beckett'll think it were me.

BLAKEY: Beckett won't get to know nowt.

CECIL: Alright Nellie!

NELLIE: (*To CECIL.*) Your lass rang.

CECIL: Oh marvellous! Lovely!

CECIL goes to the phone.

PETER: So Colin mixed a bad run of big 'olemeal?

BLAKEY: Yeah.

PETER: Are you thinking what I'm thinking?

BLAKEY: Yeah.

PETER: 'Kinnel! He wouldn't would he?

CECIL begins talking quietly on the phone, his back to the others.

BLAKEY: He took, no! – he asked me to let him take Walter off for a smoke before three.

PETER: So?

BLAKEY: I shouldn't have let him do that. It's unofficial. I can't put down in my records that any of my shift was up there before three. That mix has to go down as Nellie's or if Nellie's on a smoke...

PETER: Yours.

BLAKEY: Aye, mine.

PETER: He's a bigger bag o' shite than I thought he was.

DEZZIE: What now then Blakey?

BLAKEY: Empty the oven. Sling that burnt stuff. Walter, mix seven hours of white and one hour of 'olemeal.

DEZZIE: No half hours?

BLAKEY: Can't do it Dez, no spare wank now Colin's gone.

PETER: Good riddance.

BLAKEY: Dezzie, Lance – on the oven; Peter tinning up. We'll have Cecil go on prover changing tins.

DEZZIE: Better tek me sarnies wimme.

They all pick up their bags and cigarettes etc.

BLAKEY: Cecil! Tin change please!

CECIL: Aye, tins. (*On the phone.*) Bye, love, bye!

CECIL is bouncing up and down on his feet restlessly. He goes to pick up his bag from the table. The others look on awaiting an explanation.

What? What're you lot looking at?

PETER: What are you so chirpy about?

CECIL: Mind you're own business.

BLAKEY: Eh? What's your lass have to say Cecil?

CECIL: Marvellous. Lovely. Oh yes. Mind your own business.

PETER: (*Indicating the bouncy CECIL.*) Eh, Dezzie. Look at this will yer!

DEZZIE: Aye, he's looking lively!

PETER: Come on Cecil – cough up!

CECIL: Wonderful woman my wife. Oh yes.

DEZZIE: You're on a promise aren't yer!

CECIL: Very understanding woman. Highly valued. Oh yes.

CECIL bounces up to the bread plant with enthusiasm, mumbling to himself. The others follow. The canteen door is left open.

PETER: (*Off.*) Come on! You gorra tell us! We're your mates.

CECIL (*Off.*) It's between me and her. It's private. Oh yes.

DEZZIE (*Off.*) You can tell me Cecil, I won't tell no-one.

The lights on the plant flicker as the ovens start to turn again, accompanied by the familiar industrial thump, thump, thump. After a few moments BLAKEY enters, picks up his worksheets, and exits shutting the door behind him. Immediately he re-opens the door, looks in, and turns the lights off.

To black.

End.